Wage Policy and Long-Term Contracts

Paper $2.00   Library Edition in Cloth $3.00

JOSEPH W. GARBARINO

WAGE POLICY
AND LONG-TERM
CONTRACTS

THE BROOKINGS INSTITUTION · WASHINGTON, D.C.

THE BROOKINGS INSTITUTION is an independent organization devoted to nonpartisan research, education, and publication in economics, government, foreign policy, and the social sciences generally. Its principal purposes are to aid in the development of sound public policies and to promote public understanding of issues of national importance.

The Institution was founded December 8, 1927, to merge the activities of the Institute for Government Research, founded in 1916, the Institute of Economics, founded in 1922, and the Robert Brookings Graduate School of Economics and Government, founded in 1924.

The general administration of the Institution is the responsibility of a self-perpetuating Board of Trustees. The Trustees are also charged with maintaining the independence of the staff and fostering the most favorable conditions for creative research and education. The immediate direction of the policies, program, and staff of the Institution is vested in the President, assisted by the division directors and an advisory council, chosen from the professional staff of the Institution.

In publishing a study, the Institution presents it as a competent treatment of a subject worthy of public consideration. The interpretations and conclusions in such publications are those of the author or authors and do not necessarily reflect the views of other members of the Brookings staff or of the administrative officers of the Institution.

L 100467/AC

Foreword

ONE OF THE MOST significant developments in American industrial relations since the end of World War II has been the increasing use of the multi-year collective bargaining contract. By the end of the 1950's a large majority of the large-scale contracts in the United States were negotiated for a period of two years or more. In the transition to the multi-year contract, it was necessary to develop policies for adjusting wages during the life of the contract. To the economist, the wage policies that were developed to make the long-term contracts acceptable are of particular interest because they force management, the union, and, to some extent, the community at large, to make conscious decisions about the pattern of wage change appropriate to a changing economy.

The original and still the most interesting example of a long-term wage policy is the "wage formula" used in the 1948 agreement between the General Motors Corporation and the United Automobile Workers. In its essentials, this system is still operating in important sectors of the economy, and variations of the formula approach made up the dominant form of wage adjustment systems in the latter half of the 1950's. Although the details of the wage adjustment systems may be undergoing modification, there is every reason to believe that the problem of long-run wage policy will be at least as important in the decade to come.

In this study, Joseph W. Garbarino analyzes the forces leading to the development of the wage formula and its variations, considers the validity of this approach to a general wage policy, and examines the way it has operated in practice. The analysis is then extended to include the conditions under which this system of wage adjustment and some of the major alternative forms of collective bargaining contracts might be workable. Professor Garbarino concludes that the formula approach is not universally applicable but that under certain circumstances it can be a workable policy in particular sectors of the economy.

Perhaps the most useful conclusion is that it is unrealistic to expect changes in the form of collective bargaining settlements to alter the basic balance of bargaining power. As a result, the evaluation of any specific form of contract must involve a comparison of the probable results of available alternatives rather than a comparison with an implicitly assumed ideal system.

The Advisory Committee, comprising George W. Taylor, William G. Bowen, John T. Dunlop, Charles L. Schultze, and Albert E. Rees, made helpful comments and suggestions for improving the manuscript. Mrs. Virginia Haaga edited the manuscript and prepared the index. The author and the Institution are deeply indebted to them for their assistance.

The views expressed in this study are those of the author, and they do not necessarily represent the views of the Trustees, Officers, or other staff members of the Brookings Institution.

Robert D. Calkins
President

March 1962

Author's Acknowledgments

IN THE PREPARATION of this study, excellent co-operation was received from representatives of unions and management in a number of industries. In particular, discussions were held with management personnel in the automobile, steel, electrical machinery, and railroad industries and with representatives from the automobile, steel, and electrical unions. Some of the ideas were presented in a paper before the American Economic Association and the American Statistical Association in December 1959, and the comments on that paper of Walter D. Fackler, then of the Cabinet Committee on Price Stability and Economic Growth, and Nathaniel Goldfinger of the AFL-CIO were helpful. H. M. Douty of the Bureau of Labor Statistics was helpful in providing statistical data.

During the preparation of the study, I served as a visiting professor at the School of Industrial and Labor Relations at Cornell University, as well as on the staff of the Institute of Industrial Relations of the University of California, Berkeley, and benefited from the discussion of many points with colleagues at these institutions. In view of the occasionally trying circumstances under which the work was performed, my wife deserves substantial credit for her patience and forbearance. No one but myself, of course, can be held responsible for the final result.

Joseph W. Garbarino

March 1962
University of California
Berkeley, California

Contents

1

Introduction

WRITING IN THE middle 1950's, a vice-president of a large manufacturing company summed up his assessment of management wage policy by remarking:

> The plain truth is that management has done only a modest amount of thinking about labor. . . .
>
> Management is primarily concerned with products which are feasible to produce in large volume and at lowest possible cost, readily saleable at prices which will recapture the investment and produce a profit to reward investors and nurture a repetition of the process. This is the industrial Valhalla, constantly rebuilding by people who, like Wotan, have not thought through in advance the deal the giants will exact.[1]

This colorful description might well have applied to "management" in general at the time it was written. Some important segments of American business, however, had been attempting for several years to develop wage and collective bargaining policies that reflected long-term policy decisions. By 1959 there was ample evidence that wage policy in collective bargaining had become of prime concern to management. The 1958 contract negotiations in the automobile industry showed evidence for perhaps the first time of a relatively unified management approach to bargaining policy. The 1959 negotiations in the steel industry furnished another example in which it appeared that the highest levels of corporate leadership participated in working out a multi-company stand on the content of the current labor contracts. In a number of other industries—petroleum refining, for

[1] Leland Hazard, vice-president and general counsel, Pittsburgh Plate Glass Company, in *New Concepts in Wage Determination*, George W. Taylor and Frank C. Pierson (eds.) (McGraw-Hill, 1957), p. 49.

1

example—there was informal consultation among companies on wage policy. Whatever the situation had been previously, as the decade of the 1950's drew to a close, there was no doubt that the political and economic consequences of the price and wage decisions made in earlier years had become a matter of vital concern in the upper levels of corporate hierarchies.

One of the more important postwar trends in American industrial relations has been the emergence of the multi-year collective bargaining agreement as the typical form of contract. Since this growth is traced in some detail in Chapter 5, it is sufficient at this point to note that by the end of the 1950's, 80 to 90 per cent of the contracts covering more than 5,000 workers had a duration of two years or more (up from perhaps 20 to 25 per cent in 1948). Although the equivalent figure for contracts covering fewer than 5,000 workers is not available, it is justifiable to conclude that a substantial majority of American workers under collective bargaining contracts are currently covered by long-term agreements and have been for some years.

Important as this development is in its own right, much more significant is the fact that the trend to long-term agreements has been accompanied by, and indeed has been made possible by the development of systems of automatic wage adjustment during the life of these contracts. In recent years the great majority of multi-year agreements have included some form of wage increase scheduled in advance to take effect in the future. The economic significance of long-term contracts is much less a result of their duration than of the wage settlements contained in most of them.

To the economist and to the general public, the most interesting and important type of automatic adjustment mechanism is that which combines escalator clauses and annual wage increases in the same system. Faced with the problem of programing wage changes for several years into the future, at least some managements have been forced to give the question of long-run wage policy explicit consideration. The combination of escalator clauses and annual increases in a wage "package" was pioneered by General Motors and the United Automobile Workers (UAW) in 1948. Since that time this approach to wage determination has waxed and waned over the years, reaching its peak coverage of close to five million workers in 1958. In addition, the system influenced wage developments throughout the economy as a whole. The experiments in wage policy sparked by a desire to negotiate long-term agreements are the subject of this book.

This study starts from the assumption that the years since World War II have produced at least one important attempt to work out a coherent wage policy and to apply it in a major power center of union-management relations. This policy was embodied in the 1948 contract between the General Motors Corporation and the United Automobile Workers. In the chapters to come it is argued that the approach used in this agreement was unique in that it was an attempt to develop a policy on the substance of bargaining, as distinct from a strategy for use in the bargaining process. The cynic may question whether the official rationale of the policy was not designed to fit the mechanics of the system, rather than vice versa; but at least subsequent actions of both parties appear to have been shaped to accord with this rationale in important ways. In the pragmatic tradition of American collective bargaining, theory probably follows practice more often than not; but the official promulgation of a theory, even if *ex post facto,* can have important consequences for behavior. The significant point is that both General Motors and the United Automobile Workers publicly accepted a particular pattern of wage behavior as desirable at least during the term of particular contracts extending over as many as five years. Although some of the critical parameters in the wage-setting system intended to make the policy operative are imprecisely defined, the broad outlines of agreement are present and have been acted upon. In this study the wage policy in question is referred to as the "formula wage policy."

In its simplest form, the formula wage policy is based on the thesis that the increases in real wages (that is, money wages corrected for price changes) made possible by increases in productivity should be distributed to workers by regular increases in money wages. Historically, the American economy has functioned so as to distribute the gains of increasing productivity in this fashion over the long run. The formula wage policy calls for doing this by conscious decision.

In the GM-UAW contracts this policy is implemented by use of a wage formula that includes both a link between wage rates and the Consumer Price Index of the U. S. Bureau of Labor Statistics and an annual increase in money wages. The adjustment of average hourly wages to changes in consumer prices at quarterly intervals stabilizes the real value of the average money wage. The contract provision calling for this arrangement is usually referred to as the "escalator clause." In addition to this adjustment in the GM-UAW contracts, money wages are increased annually to raise real wages. This is referred to as the "annual improvement factor." The improvement factor is intended to reflect the increase in productivity of the economy as a whole. The wage formula is thus the contractual form through which the over-all wage policy is implemented.[2]

In the years since the negotiation of the first of the GM-UAW contracts, many other agreements that combine cost-of-living adjustments with annual increases have been negotiated in various industries. Outside of the automobile industry and the jurisdiction of the United Automobile Workers, most of these have not been based explicitly on the economic reasoning of the formula wage policy. The major difference is that the annual increases have not been directly related to productivity changes.

In forthcoming chapters the term "formula wage policy" will refer to the specific example provided by the GM-UAW contract. Contracts that include both an escalator clause and a future wage increase scheduled in advance will be referred to as "formula-type contracts," whether or not they grew out of an explicit acceptance of the principles underlying the original contract. In other words, formula-type contracts use the mechanics but not necessarily the theory of the wage formula.

This report is based on the familiar premise that collective bargaining is an evolving system for resolving conflict between organizations. The wage policy implemented by the wage formula is a technique for ordering conflict in one area of dispute and, as such, is similar to other techniques, like the grievance procedure, seniority privileges, and the representation election. This technique is evaluated both as a possible base for an economy-wide wage policy and as a special device useful in certain sectors under certain conditions. It is assessed against absolute

---

[2] It might be noted that the practice of adjusting wages to changes in the price of bread appeared several centuries ago, and in more recent years wages have been tied to the prices of commodities produced by labor (usually a raw material) or to some measure of price changes. The system analyzed in this study seems different enough in kind to justify omitting an historical survey of these earlier arrangements.

standards of economically desirable wage behavior and against relative standards of possible alternatives. The conclusion is that the formula wage policy has had an important influence on wage developments since 1948 partly through its direct impact but, more important, through its contribution to a fairly general consensus on the appropriate secular relationship between wages and prices.

As an example of wage policy in action the formula approach is at least temporarily on the wane, but it could continue to be important in certain major areas of the economy. Under various sets of assumptions (described in Chapter 6), wage formulas and their near-relatives may be superior to alternative types of collectively bargained wage settlements, may be equally serviceable, or may be inferior. It is important to realize that, like other types of collective bargaining arrangements, these contracts reflect the balance of bargaining strength of the parties. Over the long run the application of the principles of the formula wage policy may in subtle ways act to change the environment of bargaining so that the balance of bargaining power is influenced. In the short run, however, in any given negotiation the form of the contract exerts a minor, but possibly significant, influence on the outcome of the process.[3]

The argument is developed as follows:

Chapter 2 describes the strong pressures on managements of major companies to rationalize the process of collective bargaining. These pressures have led to attempts to substitute what are sometimes called analytical processes for bargaining processes in industrial relations. The wage formula is one such analytical process, its objectives being to reduce the frequency of bargaining by permitting long-term contracts to be negotiated, to narrow the range of dispute, and to achieve economically viable settlements within the framework of private dispute settlements. This approach can also be compatible with the long-range goals of the union.

Chapter 3 deals with the "feasible" (roughly speaking, noninflationary) rate of wage increase, as determined by historical rates of increase in productivity. A major problem arises from the difficulty of producing a given increase in real income per capita by changing wage

---

[3] This study is based on the assumption that collective bargaining directly influences wage behavior. The lay observer may be surprised that it is necessary to make this assumption explicit, but there is a substantial body of professional opinion that questions its validity.

rates for individual jobs. It includes a fairly elaborate attempt to estimate the feasible rate of wage increase that is appropriate to given
rates of increase in real income per capita and in productivity.

Chapter 4 considers some of the major criticisms of the formula
approach as a wage policy. It examines the difficulties of designing a
pattern of differential wage changes by occupation and industry that
will be compatible with labor market conditions while remaining
within the feasible rate of wage increase. The complications created
by competitive unionism are discussed, as is the charge that the formulas are a built-in inflationary device.

On the basis of the analysis in Chapters 3 and 4, the wage formula
is deemed unsuitable as a general wage policy, but is regarded as workable from the standpoint of both the community and individual companies if confined to prosperous companies with an above-average rate
of productivity increase and preferably with expanding employment.

In Chapter 5 the results of the formula approach to wage policy in
practice are reported and analyzed. The basic conclusion is that, during the "age of escalation" (the latter half of the decade of the fifties),
experiments in wage determination by formula were launched that
proved unsatisfactory largely because the balance of bargaining power
prevented the contracts from adhering to the principles that should
underlie the formula wage policy. One of the principal difficulties arose
out of the unions' interest in the process, as well as the results, of bargaining. Since long-term contracts that include wage formulas limit
the participation of the union in the process, a multi-year contract has
become a concession that management must bargain away from the
union by paying a price in higher settlements or, at a minimum, by ex-
pending bargaining power that might have been used to reduce the
cost of the settlement in other ways.

In Chapter 6 the formula approach is compared with some alternative forms of wage determination, and an attempt is made to specify
the conditions under which each is appropriate and to compare their
results in a given situation. The study concludes with some remarks on
the contribution of the discussion generated by the formula wage policy to the question of increasing social control of collective bargaining.

2

Long-Term Contracts and the Wage Formula

IN 1946 AN ANALYST of the collective bargaining relationships in General Motors reported as follows to a group of the corporation's executives on the findings of a committee of professors of personnel and industrial relations.[1]

> In addition to "Tough but Fair" we also concluded that the policies of the Corporation with respect to labor relations were shortsighted, unimaginative, defensive, and at times almost defeatist.

Four years later, the same analyst could say:

> In collective bargaining, GM always appears to have clear-cut objectives and a long-range plan; and, as a shrewd observer once pointed out to me, "GM has steps five and six of that plan in mind when it takes steps two and three." In bargaining it has usually been aggressive rather than defensive.

There are a number of explanations for the striking shift of opinion indicated by these two quotations. The first statement was made shortly after the conclusion of the approximately 111-day strike of 1945-46 and undoubtedly was conditioned by the bitterness and conflict in the relationship at that time. Labor relations at this period were in a state of rapid change, and the time horizons of commentators were relatively short. Over a longer period, there are some reasons for believing that the 1946 statement was not entirely fair to the General

[1] Frederick H. Harbison in *Proceedings*, Conference for College and University Educators, General Motors Corporation (1946), p. 4. The next quotation is from "The General Motors and United Auto Workers Agreement of 1950," *Journal of Political Economy* (October 1950), p. 400.

Motors management. The reversal in the evaluation of the corporation's labor policy reflects an actual change in labor relations strategy, but in part it probably also reflects some change in the perception of this strategy by an outside observer.

Even with these qualifications, there is no question, however, that dramatic changes in the relationships between General Motors and the United Automobile Workers occurred between 1946 and 1950. Concrete evidence of this change is to be found in the 1948 contract between the corporation and the union. This contract represents the most important single postwar development in industrial relations. It is the most significant attempt to deal with union-management problems on the basis of an explicit, long-range policy. The contract was notable as the first of a continuing series of multi-year agreements and for the inclusion of a wage formula designed to make feasible an extension of the contract period to several years. The keystone of this approach to collective bargaining was the wage formula, a two-part provision that called for adjustment of wage rates to changes in a price index and for annual increases in wages to raise the real value of the money wage.

As a model for collective bargaining contracts, the 1948 agreement had little influence. A second agreement, negotiated immediately prior to the outbreak of hostilities in Korea in 1950 and running for five years, attracted more attention. Interest appeared to be centered, however, as much on the unusual length of the term of its contract as on the wage provisions. With the beginning of the Korean fighting in June 1950, interest in wage agreements that scheduled wage adjustments in advance grew rapidly. Since that time the prevalence of automatic wage adjustments of one type or another has waxed and waned, but, as a rough estimate, the number of workers under one form or another has not fallen below 2 million.[2]

The great majority of these were to be found in the automobile industry and among members of the United Automobile Workers. At the high point of interest in this type of wage contract more than 5 million workers were covered by some form of multi-year contract providing for periodic wage changes specified in advance.

As will be detailed in later chapters, the waxing and waning of the

[2] Data on coverage of the various forms of adjustments of this type are given in detail in Chapter 5.

numbers covered by an automatic wage adjustment were not due entirely to fluctuations in the popularity of the particular version of this system found in the automobile industry. The GM-UAW prototype was adopted virtually unchanged by the other automobile manufacturers in 1951, shortly after the outbreak of hostilities in Korea. In the next year or two this system was extended to the other branches of industry organized by the United Automobile Workers with only minor changes. The casual observer, however, sometimes overestimates the extent to which the wage-formula policy was adopted during the Korean inflation. Either the escalator clause or the annual wage increase was fairly widely accepted, but outside the United Automobile Workers' orbit the two were combined in relatively few major contracts. The escalator clause was the more popular, but as the inflation ended, it was dropped from the great bulk of the contracts. The surge of what have been designated as "formula-type contracts" began in 1955-56, when escalator clauses and annual increases were combined in major agreements in the electrical equipment, steel, construction, railroad, trucking, and other industries. Neither managements nor the unions involved in this wave of settlements accepted productivity of the economy as a whole as the basis for the formula, and the annual increases were usually larger than those in the automobile industry.

The economic consequences of the various systems of periodic wage adjustments, originally adopted by at least some of the parties concerned as an expedient way of dealing with the short-run problems of industrial relations stability, came to be questioned with increasing frequency as the decade of the 1950's progressed. Toward the end of the fifties concern with the problems of long-term inflation and the vigorous and continuing debate as to its causes and remedies appeared to be leading to a re-examination of collective bargaining policy in general and long-term contracts providing for periodic wage adjustments in particular.

In this chapter the center of attention will be the formula wage policy in its "pure" form, as expressed in the GM-UAW agreement. The discussion begins with a review of the historical background of industrial relations from 1945 to 1948 in order to point up the forces that led to the introduction of the new system, and passes in turn to a description of the mechanics of the formula, the official rationale for its use, and a statement of the union position on the issue. The chapter closes with a brief sketch of some other management strategies of the period. Variants of the formula system are analyzed in Chapters 5 and 6.

The emphasis on the wage formula should not obscure the fact that the underlying goal of bargaining strategy in this period was to minimize industrial strife by negotiating long-term contracts. In an important sense the wage formula was the price that had to be paid for a multi-year contract without periodic reopenings. On the other hand, lengthening the term of the contract itself is of relatively little interest compared to the impact of adopting a system of wage adjustment that provides for automatic wage changes for periods ranging up to five years in the future.

There are a number of reasons for focussing attention on the formula wage policy. From the time of the first GM-UAW contract up to the present this version of the wage policy has had a formal rationale which is based on certain empirical relationships between aggregative economic data and which deals with problems that can be related to larger issues of economic policy. It is more than a method of settling a wage dispute between a specific company and a specific union. At times it has appeared to be a conscious attempt to provide a base for a general wage policy. In particular, this wage policy raises the question whether economic progress and our collective bargaining institutions will permit us to schedule continuing increases in real wages for periods of several years in advance without suffering untoward consequences. The more traditional collective bargaining practices may involve the same kinds of issues, but the mechanics of the wage formula lay the problem bare for public inspection in a much more direct and inescapable fashion.

The Evolution of a Collective Bargaining Policy

A review of the context into which the formula approach to wage policy was introduced is essential to an understanding of the pressures on management that brought about its development. The review also will help outline the goals it was expected to achieve.

As the war with Japan ended in August 1945, it was necessary to begin building a collective bargaining system for American industry under very difficult circumstances. The wartime arrangements for settling industrial relations problems involved a temporary structure intended to deal primarily with problems of dispute settlement and wage stabilization as part of a framework of over-all economic controls. This wartime pattern had been superimposed on an immature and undeveloped system of private collective bargaining that existed in 1941.

Unionism in the mass production industries in the United States dated only from 1937, the year in which General Motors recognized the UAW as the collective bargaining representative for its members after a series of dramatic sit-down strikes. In the same year the United States Steel Corporation recognized the Steel Workers' Organizing Committee, predecessor of the United Steelworkers of America, and unions were established in the rubber, electrical, and maritime industries, among others.[3] In the automobile industry, General Motors' first national agreement (that is, an agreement dealing with wages on a company-wide rather than a local plant basis) was negotiated in 1939. The Ford Motor Company did not recognize the United Automobile Workers as bargaining agent for its employees until 1941.

By 1941 almost 8.5 million workers were union members, more than double the 4 million members in 1936 and almost three times the approximately 3 million enrolled in 1933.[4] As a result, when the control agencies took over in 1942, the institutions and practices of collective bargaining were new to the great majority of union members, their officers, and the company officials with whom they dealt. Union growth continued during the war in an atmosphere of increasing friction until in 1945 American employers and a powerful union movement of about 12.7 million members faced the difficult problems of reconversion with very little experience in "free" collective bargaining. An attempt to ease the transition to peacetime bargaining through the device of a President's Labor-Management Conference in 1945 failed to improve matters, and the industrial relations situation deteriorated rapidly.

During 1945, man-days lost through strikes exceeded the previous high point of 1937, and an all-time record was set in 1946, when strikers

[3] W. H. McPherson, chapter on "Automobiles," and Frederick H. Harbison, chapter on "Steel," in *How Collective Bargaining Works* (Twentieth Century Fund, 1942).

[4] Membership figures are from Irving Bernstein, "The Growth of American Trade Unions," *American Economic Review* (June 1954).

were idle a total of 116 million man-days. During the month of February 1946 alone, it was estimated that strikers were off the job a total of 23 million man-days, the equivalent of more than a million workers for the entire month's working days.[5] During 1945-46, 200,000 General Motors employees struck for some 111 days; about 450,000 workers in basic steel were out for over 24 days; 174,000 electrical workers were on strike against General Motors, Westinghouse, and General Electric for various periods up to several months; and three major coal strikes occurred, involving between 200,000 and 340,000 miners and lasting 17 to 59 days. The impact of these disputes was greatly intensified by widespread shortages of goods resulting from wartime conditions.

The search for a method of dealing with disputes of this magnitude led to adoption of the fact-finding board device. Under this approach *ad hoc* boards of prominent citizens with industrial relations experience were named by the President to hear the "facts" and make recommendations for settlement. The first two such boards to report—the petroleum industry and the General Motors boards—set a pattern for the postwar "first round" of wage increases that was confirmed when President Truman recommended an 18.5-cent wage increase for the steel industry. Fact-finding boards were named in a number of other important strikes during this period, and President Truman is reported to have proposed a law calling for permanent fact-finding machinery in major disputes.[6] When the Taft-Hartley Act was passed in 1947, it included a section dealing with national emergency strikes through fact-finding by boards of inquiry, but these boards did not have power to recommend a settlement.

Although by 1947 large-scale industrial strife was confined to the troubled coal industry, the contemporary record suggests that the reaction of at least some members of the management community to the hectic postwar period might be summed up as follows:

1. There was a need to develop regularized institutions and practices that would channel and contain labor-management conflict so as to permit orderly settlement of issues in dispute. This meant procedures to institutionalize conflicts during the negotiation of new contracts, as well as those arising during the term of the contracts.

[5] Strike data from U.S. Bureau of Labor Statistics, *Handbook of Labor Statistics,* 1950 edition, Bulletin No. 1016 (1951), pp. 158-62.
[6] *Business Week* (Dec. 8, 1945), pp. 17-18.

2. It was important that the achievement of order and system in procedures not be purchased at too high a price in terms of economic concessions or in the reduction of the area of management authority.[7] For many companies this problem was complicated by the fact that, under the pressure for wartime production, many forms of internal control over work practices and standards and wage schedules had eroded. These companies felt the necessity of embarking on a slow and difficult process of tightening performance standards.

3. It was clear that a failure to achieve reasonable success in stabilizing labor-management relations would mean an extension of government participation in the processes of collective bargaining and further sharing of managerial authority with government officials as well as with labor leaders.

In the case of General Motors most of these problems presented themselves in particularly acute form. Not only was the corporation a massive industrial complex and a highly visible political and industrial relations target, but it was a recognized leader in management philosophy and practice. In addition, the corporation had been at the center of the postwar strife. Although General Motors dealt with more than twenty different national unions, the overwhelming majority of its organized employees were members of the United Automobile Workers, with a sizeable, though relatively small, minority (about 10 per cent) in the United Electrical, Radio and Machine Workers Union. On many issues the latter union followed a militant left-wing policy that was to lead to its expulsion after the 1948 presidential election from the Congress of Industrial Organizations on charges of Communist domination. The United Automobile Workers was an aggressive union, split by factionalism and with a fairly sizeable radical group in its ranks. In the immediate postwar years the then president of the union, R. J. Thomas, was being challenged for leadership by Walter Reuther. Reuther had been active in the 1937 organizing strikes against General Motors and was campaigning against Thomas from a base as head of the General Motors Department of the United Automobile Workers. In addition to his activity in the internal politics of

[7] General Motors has always placed great stress on the clause found in each of its wage-formula contracts (in 1948, 1950, 1955, 1958, and 1961) stating that "a continuing improvement in the standard of living of employes (sic) depends upon technological progress, better tools, methods, processes, and equipment, and a cooperative attitude on the part of all parties in such process."

the labor movement, Reuther was an outspoken advocate of more aggressive government action in a variety of economic and social affairs and was forceful and adept in bringing his views to public attention.

At the time of the long General Motors strike in 1945-46 Reuther made a major issue of a proposal that the corporation "open the books" to enable the union to show that the wage increases demanded would not require offsetting price increases. When it appeared that the General Motors fact-finding board would consider "ability to pay" in its hearings, the company withdrew from the proceedings.[8]

General Motors had already demonstrated an awareness of the need to systematize its labor-management relations and a willingness to experiment in attacking the problem. The 1941 contract negotiated with the UAW had introduced a formal grievance procedure culminating in outside arbitration into collective bargaining contracts in the durable goods industries.[9] Grievance procedures provide an alternative to economic force in deciding conflicts that arise in the day-to-day administration of a collective bargaining contract. Typically the company and the union agree to maintain the status quo while a dispute passes through a series of appeals moving up through company and union organizational levels until a settlement is reached or the case is decided by an arbitrator. In one form or another, a grievance procedure can be found in almost all contracts today.

In addition to pioneering formal grievance procedures in large-scale industry, GM was more successful than the average company in resisting the trend toward the loosening of performance standards during the war years.[10] It should be noted that, anxious as GM has been to minimize interruptions to production during the life of its union contracts, for many years the only type of dispute which the corporation insisted could not be taken to arbitration through the grievance procedure (and thus determined by outsiders) was a conflict over work standards or the associated wage rates. In any battle over the setting of

[8] *Business Week* (Jan. 1, 1946), p. 96.

[9] Charles E. Wilson, former president of the corporation, has stated that this development grew out of a conversation with Sidney Hillman, then president of the Amalgamated Clothing Workers. The garment industries had had long experience with grievance procedures. General Motors Corporation, *Fourth Conference for College and University Educators*, First Session (June 16, 1948), p. 5.

[10] Frederick H. Harbison and Robert Dubin, *Patterns of Union Management Relations* (Science Research Associates, 1947), p. 49. Part II of this study contains an excellent review of the GM-UAW relationship.

a production standard, the union retained the right to strike during the term of the contract. In a study published in 1947 two students of industrial relations characterized the General Motors collective bargaining policy up to that date as one of "containment,"[11] and most observers would probably agree with that description. This suggests that the wage-formula approach in the 1948 contract is analogous to the role of the grievance procedure in contract administration. As the grievance procedure "contains" conflict during the life of the contract, the wage formula tends to contain conflict over wages when new contracts are negotiated by structuring at least part of the issues in disagreement and suggesting criteria for settlement.

The language of organization theory provides another way of expressing this version of the evolution of managerial policy. In discussing conflict within an organization, writers on organization theory distinguish between two sets of methods of resolving conflict, and these concepts appear to be applicable to interorganizational conflict as well. The two types of procedure are referred to as analytic processes and bargaining processes.[12] Analytic processes are those that try to secure private as well as public agreement to the decisions that are reached, while bargaining processes imply public agreement only. In other words, analytic methods require agreement on the criteria to be applied in resolving disputes rather than the mere acceptance of a settlement. As techniques for resolving conflict, both the grievance procedure and the wage formula are efforts to substitute analytic processes for bargaining processes. They attempt to achieve agreement in principle on methods of settling disputes and standards to be applied in their settlement. In the case of the grievance procedure a series of successive appeal steps are involved with arbitration as the final step. The standards to be applied are conformance with the terms of the written agreement or with existing practices and precedents as the latter have evolved over the years. In the case of the wage formula the methods involve scheduled wage adjustments to offset changes in prices and to raise levels of living. The standards used are price changes as measured

[11] "The nub of the General Motors labor relations policy has been to contain unions. . . ." The same, p. 46. Harbison saw the 1950 agreement as part of this process in "The General Motors and United Auto Workers Agreement of 1950," pp. 401-02.

[12] James G. March and Herbert A. Simon, *Organizations* (John Wiley and Sons, 1958), pp. 129-31.

by movements in the Consumer Price Index and the estimated increase in productivity for the economy as a whole. However the evolution of policy outlined here is described, it seems clear that powerful forces were pressing American management in general, and General Motors management in particular, to work out long-range policies in industrial relations.

Reinforcing these questions of over-all strategy were some important tactical considerations all of which emphasized the desirability of minimizing conflict over the terms of new contracts. For better or worse, collective bargaining negotiations at major power centers in the American economy sometimes take on the characteristics of an elaborate public spectacle. Months before the expiration of an existing contract the union, and sometimes the company, begins a campaign designed to bring its prospective demands to the attention of both the public and its own membership. Public announcements are made, "wage policy" conferences are convened, pamphlets are written and distributed, and most of the techniques of mass communication are brought into play.[13] During this period the company may conduct its own public campaign, or it may confine itself to rebuttal of union claims, but at a minimum it must face constant pressure from communication media for official high level statements on the issues raised. As the opening of negotiations draws near, the company must begin to develop its own bargaining position and must try to anticipate demands from the union. In practice this may mean gathering information on the way the current contract is working out, soliciting proposals for changes, reviewing grievances and arbitration awards, and consulting specialists on a variety of social security issues, such as pensions and health plans. As formal negotiations open (typically some sixty days before expiration of the contract), the company often finds itself confronted with an array of dozens of proposed contract changes. For example, the number of demands for contract changes proposed to GM by the UAW in 1948 is usually given as 132.[14] It is difficult for a company in this position to avoid the necessity for preparing a careful coun-

---

[13] Perhaps the outstanding example of this procedure was the excellently managed two-year campaign of the UAW for a form of wage guarantee prior to the 1955 automobile negotiations.

[14] Because of the way in which changes are proposed, this figure overstates the true number of substantive changes. See B. M. Selekman, S. K. Selekman, and S. Fuller, *Problems in Labor Relations* (McGraw-Hill, 1950), pp. 365-66.

ter argument that may involve collection of major amounts of data for each demand.

As negotiations approach the deadline, the cumulative effect of the campaign frequently shows itself in reduced efficiency on the job and possible "spontaneous" short strikes or slowdowns. In a major negotiation the deadline date often is preceded by marathon sessions involving top-level management personnel, after which an agreement is reached, a temporary extension is negotiated, or a strike is called. The actual signing of a new agreement does not end the process since the new provisions must be analyzed, actions to implement them must be taken, and supervisory personnel must be trained to administer them.

This review of a typical major collective bargaining negotiation is meant to emphasize the demands it imposes on management time and effort and the potential for reduced productivity and intra-organizational conflict that are created. If this process were repeated annually, during a substantial part of each year industrial relations problems would be occupying most of the time of a large part of an organization, and instability would be chronic.[15]

Long-term contracts are frequently described as introducing an element of stability into the collective bargaining relationship. The above account points up the fact that stability means more than predictability of wage costs and the absence of strikes. It also means minimum disruption of the normal operations of the functional divisions of the business enterprise and of the important day-to-day relationships between the company and the union and the company and its employees. The way in which the daily activities of supervision and contract administration can be important to efficiency of operation is illustrated by the substantial differences in labor efficiency that often exist among companies operating under virtually identical general collective bargaining contracts.

Under these circumstances it is hardly surprising that management has acted to provide itself with long-term policies and has sought to lengthen intervals between the occasions when these policies are tested in contract negotiations. The first step in this process was the introduction of the multi-year contract, with annual reopenings limited to

---

[15] For a good discussion of some of the considerations involved in the positions of both labor and management, see Jack Stieber, "Evaluation of Long-Term Contracts," in Harold Davey et al. (eds.), *New Dimensions in Collective Bargaining* (Harper, 1959).

specified questions such as wages or employment security. Since this did not eliminate the possibility of annual breakdowns in contract relationships, it was natural to try to work out multi-year settlements that did not include periodic reopenings. To meet this need the practice was introduced of scheduling wage changes during the life of a long-term contract. The most significant method of scheduling wage changes that resulted was the GM-UAW system as implemented through the wage formula.

To sum up: the formula wage policy is part of an over-all collective bargaining policy designed to deal with an industrial relations situation marked by powerful, aggressive unions relatively inexperienced in collective bargaining. The general policy was intended to institutionalize labor-management conflict in a form that retained the essential areas of management authority. The terms of the accommodation that developed and the means by which this accommodation was reached had to be such as to minimize governmental intervention. In the area of contract negotiation a policy of lengthening the term of agreements was adopted, and in the circumstances of the time this meant that some programming of wage changes was necessary. The GM-UAW wage formula and its variants represent the most thoroughly articulated system of programming a wage policy that resulted.

The Mechanics of the Wage Formula

In the previous sections the pressures generated by the environment of industrial relations in the years following World War II were depicted as pushing the participants in collective bargaining toward the development of long-term policies in wage negotiations. At this point the original pattern-setting policy will be outlined and its mechanics described. The GM-UAW system will be described, with emphasis on the premises on which it was based and the objectives it was expected to attain, according to the testimony of its corporate sponsors.

Because American management operates within an elaborate framework of formal and informal institutions, the task of examining the public rationale of management policies is greatly simplified. The executives of a company introducing a major policy innovation may be asked to explain the departure from generally accepted practice. These explanations are presented in business periodicals, meetings of luncheon or dinner groups, meetings of trade associations, university institutes and conferences, and on occasion congressional hearings. The same situation prevails for any major union that negotiates a novel agreement. The newsworthy character of experiments in industrial relations policies since World War II has ensured that major developments, such as the GM-UAW wage-formula contracts of 1948 and 1950, have been subject to large-scale public discussion by their protagonists. This review of the theory of the wage formula as developed by the management of General Motors, is based on the exposition of this approach to wage determination presented on numerous occasions by company spokesmen.[16] The variations of the formula approach adopted by other companies and unions have seldom had their philosophy so fully outlined. They have been cases of simple pattern following or by implication have been based on the same line of reasoning.

As already noted, the GM-UAW wage formula consists of two distinct parts. The first is the escalator clause proper or the wage-price adjustment. The second is the wage-productivity adjustment or, in the language of the GM-UAW contract, the annual improvement factor.

The escalator clause is designed to stabilize the purchasing power of money wage rates over the term of the contract. This stabilization of real wages is accomplished by making periodic adjustments in money wage rates so that the ratio between an appropriate price index and money wages at some point in time is kept constant. In the original version of the wage formula in the 1948 contract this ratio was such that a 1-cent change in GM's average hourly earnings would offset each change of 1.14 points in the Bureau of Labor Statistics' Consumer Price Index.[17]

In the GM-UAW contracts, wage rates are adjusted quarterly. There

---

[16] An accessible version of a typical presentation can be found in the contribution of Charles E. Wilson, then president of GM, to a series of public lectures published in Anne P. Cook (ed.), *Mature Collective Bargaining: Prospects and Problems* (Institute of Industrial Relations, University of California, 1952), pp. 56-72.

[17] In the spring of 1948 the BLS Consumer Price Index stood at 169.3 (old index), average hourly earnings in General Motors were $1.485, and 169.3/148.5 cents equalled 1.14. N. M. Borts and J. C. Nix, "Recently Bargained Cost-of-Living Wage Adjustments," *Monthly Labor Review* (November 1959), p. 559.

Note that the value of the ratio varies with the absolute level of the price index at the time the calculation is made and with the level of average hourly earnings in the company or industry to which the system is to be applied.

is no ceiling on the upward adjustment of wage rates, but the successive contracts have always set a floor to reductions due to price declines, a floor that has moved upward as base rates have risen. Since the original 1948 agreement, the gross wage rate in General Motors has included a base rate and a separate cost-of-living allowance. Five cents of the wage increase given at the beginning of the 1948 contract period was designated as cost-of-living allowance. The cost-of-living adjustments have been cumulated since that time, and periodically a portion of the total has been "frozen" into the base rate as part of a negotiated wage settlement. Regardless of the size of any price decline, basic wage rates cannot be reduced—only the cumulated cost-of-living allowance that has not been included in base rates is vulnerable. Over the years the amount subject to erosion in a price decline in any quarter has been as much as 26 cents and as little as 3 cents. Through 1961, the existence of the lower limit had at no time prevented a drop in wages that would otherwise have occurred.

How effectively escalator clauses maintain real earnings in the face of price changes depends on the frequency with which adjustments in rates are made, the size of the change in the Consumer Price Index that is needed to trigger a change in wage rates, and the degree of compensation for price changes. As long as it operates above the wage floor set by the basic rates, the GM-UAW version is very effective on all of these counts. The maximum lag in wage changes that can develop is one quarter, wage rates are changed in response to small changes in prices (in the 1958 contract 0.5 of a point in the Consumer Price Index), and, with some qualifications, changes in earnings completely compensate for price changes.[18]

The second part of the wage formula, the annual improvement factor, calls for an annual increase in basic wage rates, usually on the anniversary date of the contract. Since the escalator clause regularly adjusts money wage rates to offset any changes in prices that may have occurred, the annual improvement factor provides a guaranteed increase in the purchasing power of an hour's pay, that is, in the real hourly wage. As the formula was originally computed, the annual im-

---

[18] Since escalator wage adjustments are made in cents per hour, based on the ratio of the Consumer Price Index to average earnings, persons receiving below-average wage rates are over-compensated for price changes, and those receiving above average rates are under compensated

provement factor was set at 3 cents an hour, which was 2 per cent of the average hourly earnings in the corporation at the time the contract was negotiated. The 2-per cent factor was an estimate of the economy-wide rate of increase in productivity that had been achieved in past periods. In the five-year contract signed in 1950 the improvement factor was raised to 4 cents, the "living document" supplemental agreement in 1953 raised the factor to 5 cents, while each of the three-year agreements signed in 1955, 1958, and 1961 set the factor at 2½ per cent or 6 cents, whichever is greater. The shift from an improvement factor stated in cents per hour to one stated in percentage terms is in accord with the logic of the system and, more important, acts to preserve the relative positions of the various jobs in the internal rate structure.

The Rationale of the Wage Formula

Although there is no indication that the GM-UAW formula was directly inspired by academic thinking on appropriate wage policy, the notion of a long-range wage adjustment system relating wages to changes in productivity in the economy as a whole was in the air during the first postwar years. In a paper read at the annual meeting of the American Economic Association at the end of 1946, Abba P. Lerner suggested an ingenious national wage policy based on the proposition that:

> Starting from some initial set of wage rates, such as the prevailing rates, wages in general can be raised by 1 per cent about every four months (on account of the secular growth in labor productivity), without the general level of costs and prices having to rise. . . .[19]

In a book published in 1947, Alvin H. Hansen advanced a proposal in language very similar to that used later by Charles E. Wilson in his speeches explaining the adoption of the wage formula.

> In some industries it should be possible to include in the collective bargaining agreement provision for a systematic schedule for wage increases based on over-all productivity trends. This schedule should be subject to

---

[19] Abba P. Lerner, "Money as a Creature of the State," *American Economic Review* (May 1947), pp. 312-17. As far as the author knows, this is the first appearance in print of a proposal that Professor Lerner has made at frequent intervals. It is also contained in his testimony before the Joint Economic Committee of the U.S. Congress in 1959.

periodic reviews. There is no good reason why wages should always move upward by leaps and jerks. This movement makes a rational price policy difficult. If a systematic upward-moving schedule of wage increases were instituted, based on the general gains in productivity for the economy as a whole, then also a continuous pricing program could be instituted designed to give consumers their share in exceptional cost-reducing improvements through lower prices.[20]

It would not be difficult to multiply these examples.[21] Of course the proposition that wage behavior, particularly real wage behavior, is or should be related to productivity antedates the postwar years. What was new was that the contemporary proposals were prescriptive in nature and were relatively detailed. They were advanced as serious suggestions for the conduct of businesses or as a foundation for governmental policy.

Given the obvious importance of wage policy in the economic ferment of the reconversion period, it is not surprising that economists, many of them fresh from administrative posts in wartime agencies, should have advanced solutions to one of the pressing problems of the day. What is surprising is that a major corporation and a major union actually placed into effect a wage policy that, if not drawn directly from the proposals of the academicians, at least rested on the same bases and used much of the same logic.

According to the official version, the origin of the ideas behind the GM-UAW wage formula goes back to an extended hospital stay by General Motors President Charles E. Wilson while recuperating from a broken hip during the winter of 1941-42.[22] During his enforced idleness Mr. Wilson is reported to have pondered the question "What can we do to develop some kind of a formula that will take out of negotiations this continuous threat of strikes and disruption?" Recognizing that the cost-of-living adjustment alone pegs living standards, the idea of combining a progressive increase in the standard of living with the

---

[20] Alvin H. Hansen, *Economic Policy and Full Employment* (McGraw-Hill, 1947), p. 247.

[21] John T. Dunlop reports several in "Productivity and the Wage Structure," in *Income, Employment and Public Policy* (W. W. Norton, 1948), pp. 341-42 and provides an example himself in *American Wage Determination; The Trend and Its Significance* (U.S. Chamber of Commerce, January 1947), p. 14.

[22] This review is based on the account by GM Vice-President, Harry Anderson, in *Proceedings, Sixth Conference for College and University Educators* (General Motors Corporation, August 1950), p. 3.

protection against price changes provided by cost-of-living changes was developed. Research by the General Motors staff into the rate of increase in living standards led to the selection of the 2-per cent annual rate of increase as "the average for the country as a whole." This figure was adopted only after "he (Wilson) was quite satisfied that we (GM) could do better than 2 per cent annually."

From this general concept the specific wage formula outlined in the previous section was developed. In the course of this development and in the debate that followed negotiation of the 1948 and the 1950 contracts, a fairly complete and economically sophisticated argument for the formula pattern of wage behavior was built up.

The case for the formula rests on two lines of argument. One is that it really changes only the form of wage determination, not the substance. It is argued that a study of general wage trends in the past shows that movements in money wages and prices have tended to compensate the worker for changes in the general price level and also to increase real wages at approximately the 2- or 2½-per cent rate provided for in the formulas.

Perhaps the most extreme statement of this position is the following from a Wilson speech:

> I have a chart showing actual average wages in all manufacturing from 1910 to date, also what those wages would have been if the GM-UAW formula had been adopted in all industries in 1910, when the average wage was 20 cents an hour. You will note that by the formula the average wage would now be $1.50 per hour instead of $1.60 per hour, which it actually is. You will note the conformity between the actual and the calculated wage for more than 40 years. The chart also shows what the average wage would be today if the formula had been adopted in 1940, a little over 10 years ago. You will note that the calculated wages would be one cent of today's actual wages. However, any employer and union which had agreed on such a formula in 1940 would certainly have saved a lot of friction and strikes during the last 10 years.[23]

This pragmatic reliance on past experience was supplemented by a more elaborate statement of the relationship that should exist among wages, prices, and productivity in an economically progressive society. In this statement General Motors adopted what is probably the position of most American economists on how to distribute the gains re-

[23] Quoted in David Levinson, "The Meaning of Productivity in Wage Negotiations," *Labor Law Journal* (January 1959), p. 47.

sulting from increased efficiency. Stated in its simplest terms, this position is that in an economy that is enjoying a secular rise in its real income, this rise should be distributed by raising money incomes with stable prices rather than by stabilizing average incomes and reducing prices.[24]

Both GM officials and economists generally conduct their discussion of wage-price-productivity behavior in the context of certain assumptions. These typically include projection of past increases in productivity into the indefinite future unless there are clear reasons for not doing so, acceptance of the desirability of price stability or, at a minimum, of the avoidance of secular inflation, achievement of high levels of employment over the long run, and continuance of approximately the present distribution of the national income among the various functional shares (for example, wages, profits, rent, interest, and so on).

Considering the two parts of the wage formula in turn, Mr. Wilson has summed up General Motors' position on the cost-of-living adjustment in this way:

> In itself it is neither inflationary nor deflationary. It simply adjusts the wages of our employees after the fact to what inflationary pressures have forced on the national economy . . .
>
> . . . Where there are organized groups and frozen wage contracts are involved, crises are always created if the cost-of-living rises rapidly during the period of such a contract. Under such circumstances dissatisfaction and unrest mounts, efficiency declines, and a big issue develops when the contract expires. In such situations wages are adjusted by the pressure of bargaining, with a great deal of antagonism in the process and frequently resulting in bitter strikes.
>
> . . . Our formula is designed to accomplish this inevitable adjustment smoothly, in a manner which avoids the friction inherent in the old method. . . .

Turning to the annual improvement factor, Wilson defended a policy of increasing money wages faster than prices as the method of distributing gains in productivity:

> . . . The principle of annual improvement in real wages based on technology we also hold to be neither inflationary nor deflationary. It does

[24] One of many statements of the reasons for choosing the first alternative can be found in John C. Davis and Thomas K. Hitch, "Wages and Productivity," *Review of Economics and Statistics* (November 1949). For an opposing view see P. T. Kilsworth, "From Dollar Shortage to Dollar Glut," *Michigan Business Review* (March 1960), p. 14.

share promptly with workmen part of the fruits of technology. Unit costs are not supposed to increase since productivity is assumed to increase at least as fast as hourly wages. . . . Therefore, no price increases should result from such wage increases. On the other hand, the purchasing power of the dollar would tend to be stabilized instead of increased, as would be the case if wages were held down and prices reduced and there were no inflationary pressures. Furthermore, there is no good ethical or economic reason for asking workmen and current producers to forego all economic gain in order to increase the purchasing power of all the wealth accumulated in past years.[25]

The GM exposition of the economics of the wage formula, as recorded in the literature on the subject, might be recapitulated as follows: Increases in productivity can be expected in the future that will permit the standard of living of the population to increase. These increases should be realized through higher incomes, including higher wage rates. If real wages are raised at the same average rate as productivity increases, there should be no increase in unit costs and no need for prices to rise. Since *real* wages are to be raised, money wages must be adjusted to offset price changes and to provide for the real wage increase through the improvement factor. Considering the economy as a whole, this wage policy is neutral in its effects on prices since unit costs are assumed not to increase as a result of operation of the improvement factor. By itself the annual improvement factor increase would not bring the escalator into operation. If inflation arises from some other source, there is no obvious reason why the burden should fall on the workers, and through their organizations they would probably effectively resist a reduction in their real wages anyway. The primary effect of the cost-of-living adjustment is thus to minimize the social conflict involved in adjusting to non-wage-induced inflation. The improvement factor for its part provides for the orderly adjustment of living standards to increases in productivity in an equitable and economically desirable way and permits the negotiation of long-term labor contracts, which contribute to industrial peace and social stability.

[25] Cook (ed.), *Mature Collective Bargaining*, pp. 59-61.

Union Bargaining Policy

Omission of any discussion of union collective bargaining policy to this point is not meant to imply that such policies do not exist or are unimportant. It is not hard to find examples of union bargaining tactics that appear to have been designed to produce a series of settlements each of which moves consistently toward a definite goal. For example, the great majority of innovations in collective bargaining contracts are prepared for over successive negotiations. The history of the guaranteed wage issue illustrates the evolution of a goal from the status of a "blue sky" demand to that of an at least partially accomplished fact. This history runs at least from the 1943 demand of the Steelworkers' union to the 1955 Ford-UAW negotiation of the current supplementary unemployment benefit plan. The union security issue provides other examples. A typical pattern of development in this area would involve recognition of the union as exclusive bargaining agent for all employees, then as exclusive bargaining agent with the addition of some form of maintenance-of-membership provision, followed by a modified union shop, and, finally, the full union shop.

As far as the wage formula is concerned, however, the development of the formal system and the timing of its introduction appear to have been the contribution of the management of General Motors. No evidence has been found that the Automobile Workers or any other union ever proposed an explicit wage adjustment system of this type.

When General Motors negotiators proposed the wage formula, however, they pointed out that it provided a means of meeting generalized wage objectives that have been expressed by the union on numerous occasions. The wage formula was originally presented to the union in a written statement delivered May 21, 1948.[26] This statement contained the following paragraph:

> The union now and in the past has interpreted the worker's problem as a dual one:
> a. The problem of maintaining the purchasing power of an hour of work —in other words, protecting the worker from increases in consumer prices.

[26] The text of the statement is reproduced in Selekman, Selekman, and Fuller, *Problems in Labor Relations*, pp. 368-70.

b. The problem of assuring the worker that the buying power of his hour of work will increase as the nation's industrial efficiency improves.

The union has indicated that its economic demands were designed to deal with both of these objectives.

The leaders of the Automobile Workers would argue that this interpretation of their wage policy is incomplete. To the two principles of wage policy mentioned in the quotation, they would add a third—that their policy aims not only at increasing the real wages of the workers at a rate equivalent to the improvement in the nation's industrial efficiency but also at increasing the workers' share of national income. Under the usual assumptions in this type of discussion, this additional goal implies increasing the real wage faster than industrial efficiency rises.

Since the adoption of the wage-formula approach in 1948, spokesmen for the union have described this formula as a "springboard for progress." According to this interpretation, the auto industry wage policy provides at least in a rough way for maintenance of the status quo with respect to the division of national income. (This assumes that the proper improvement factor is included and ignores the possibility of shifts in employment.) With this much assured, the union is free to use its bargaining position when the contract is renegotiated to try to increase the workers' share of the total income either by negotiating an additional wage increment or by adding some nonwage benefit to the contract.

This view of the significance of the wage formula and its relationship to the wage policy of the United Automobile Workers is elaborated in the following statement:[27]

Our Union does not regard the present distribution of national income as between workers and other groups as either equitable or workable.

It is not equitable because it does not provide the workers with the living standards that the high productivity of the American economy makes possible. It is not workable because the inability of workers to consume proportionately to their production periodically plunges the economy into depressions. . . .

From our standpoint, the major significance of the escalator and improvement-factor wage formula is that it avoids the necessity for workers repeatedly to dissipate their militancy and their organized power in recur-

[27] Provided by Nat Weinberg, Director, Special Projects and Economic Analysis, United Automobile Workers, in a letter to the writer (Jan. 22, 1960).

rent struggles to restore living standards undermined by inflation, and to keep pace with the growth in the total national product resulting from technological advance.

The escalator provides anti-inflationary protection. The improvement factor, if it were larger, would serve to maintain intact, during the life of an agreement, the workers' share in the growing output of our expanding economy. Thus, if the principles of this wage formula are properly applied, workers can be assured of having, at the expiration of each agreement, higher living standards than they had at the time of its signing, and a share in the total national product at least as large as they had at the time the agreement was signed.

They would therefore be free to concentrate in their negotiations for a new agreement on the major objective of increasing their share in the total national product. The entire power of their trade union organizations could be devoted to this basic purpose.

It is thus clear that the formula wage policy provides a partial response to union wage policy as this policy is interpreted by management. The goals of making up for price increases and of providing for a share in the gains of increasing productivity are standard wage aims of many unions. In this generalized form they are compatible with a broad range of collective bargaining policies. There is no evidence that the wage-formula approach had ever been considered by the UAW or any other union. Hence, this chapter treats the formula technique as a management innovation and concentrates on the pressures that led to its development.

The position expressed in the union statement indicates the need for some qualification of the statement that the United Auto Workers accepted the wage formula approach "in principle." Strictly speaking, the Automobile Workers' acceptance of the principle is limited to the duration of any specific contract. In new negotiations the area of dispute expands beyond the limits of the formula. It should be noted, however, that in practice the union has not argued for increasing the worker's share of national income as vigorously as might be expected in view of the language of the statement. More typically, the union has advanced the claim that economy-wide productivity has increased more rapidly in recent years—an argument clearly within the ground rules of the wage formula. It is perhaps significant that in answer to a request for a citation on the "springboard for progress" argument, it was necessary to refer to an article in the European edition of the *CIO News,* in which the quotation originally appeared. The bargaining record, however, clearly substantiates the UAW's intention to improve on the formula at the opportunities presented by contract renewals whenever their bargaining power permits.

If General Motors is to be given credit for the invention of the wage formula, however, there is little question but that the union embraced the concept wholeheartedly and is responsible for the spread of the system throughout virtually its entire jurisdiction. In fact, it will be pointed out later that the area of application of the system during most of the period 1950-55 was nearly coterminous with the jurisdiction of the UAW in autos, auto parts, aircraft, and farm equipment. These facts clearly indicate that, although General Motors originated the formula approach, the United Automobile Workers has been the agent introducing it into other areas of its jurisdiction.

Other Management Approaches

The emphasis given to the formula wage policy in the preceding section is not intended to give the impression that no other approaches were being tried by other management groups operating in the same environment. Two major examples of other types of policies adopted in response to the exigencies of the times may be cited.

Insofar as conscious management programs are concerned, in 1945 the business community regarded the strategy of the negotiators for the Ford Motor Company as the really new element in the automobile industry's labor-relations picture. The postwar reorganization of Ford included a complete reorientation of the company's labor relations activity. In the first peacetime contract negotiations, the Ford negotiating team under John Bugas attracted considerable attention by presenting the union with demands for concessions to be made to the company. In contrast to General Motors, in its first contract in 1941 Ford had granted the United Automobile Workers a union shop and established a substantially different industrial relations system, particularly with regard to the method of representing workers through the steward system. By the end of the war the company felt that major changes would be needed to improve labor discipline and efficiency if it was to prosper in the postwar period. The demands made on the union were intended to permit the company to achieve higher productivity, to reduce the costs of the steward system, and, perhaps most important of all, to introduce company security against union irresponsibility as a counterpart to union security in the form of the compulsory membership provided by the union shop provision.

Demands of this general form continued to be made by Ford management in subsequent negotiations. Neither Ford nor Chrysler followed General Motors' lead in 1948 in adopting the wage formula, both companies signing two-year contracts with annual reopenings. Only after the outbreak of hostilities in Korea did the rest of the automobile industry negotiate formula-type contracts along with substantial numbers of other companies at the time. This marked the end of separate policies (as far as wage settlements are concerned) in the automobile industry. The pre-Korean management strategy, of which Ford offers an example, was to adopt an aggressive bargaining posture while continuing annual wage bargaining in the hope that the economic environment might change so as to increase management's bargaining power. The post-1948 wage-formula approach of General Motors on the other hand, concedes certain wage adjustments in advance as a matter of policy.

A more elaborate example of an alternative bargaining strategy is provided by the General Electric Company. In 1947 Lemuel R. Boulware was named vice-president in charge of employee, community, and union relations for General Electric. In this post Boulware developed a set of industrial relations policies that were effective enough and distinctive enough to raise the possibility that his name might acquire a kind of immortality in labor relations circles. As a strategy in labor-management affairs "Boulwareism" represented a well-thought-out attempt to develop a long-term approach to both employee and union relations and to effect a strategic combination of the two.[28]

In brief, Boulwareism involves a continuing program of direct company communication with employees on a wide variety of topics, including current and prospective issues in collective bargaining. In collective bargaining, the more spectacular aspect of the technique, the company meets with the union to discuss union demands and then at an appropriate time advances what it believes to be a fair proposal. From the union point of view the element of low cunning in the pro-

[28] For a discussion of this strategy, see Robert McMurray, "War and Peace in Industrial Relations," Harvard Business Review (November-December 1955).

cedure is that the offer actually may be very close to the anticipated final settlement. Having made what it declares to be its final offer, the company announces a date at which it will be placed into effect for all unorganized workers and for any union that accepts it and asserts that any settlement reached after that date will not be made retroactive. The company's proposal is widely publicized to its employees, and an effort is made to build up grassroots pressure on the union leadership for its acceptance. In essence, the strategy is designed to minimize the role of the union in bargaining and particularly to undercut the image of the union as the indispensable champion of employee interests against a grasping employer. Under certain circumstances this technique has worked with enough success to be imitated frequently.

Examples of other types of management strategy could be given, but these two illustrate the basic difference between the majority of these approaches and the GM-UAW wage policy: With the general acceptance of unionism and collective bargaining as relatively permanent features of the American economy, a great many management groups have attempted to evolve some sort of policy in union-management relations. Like the Ford and General Electric examples, almost all of these strategies have been concerned primarily with the process rather than the substance of collective bargaining. Insofar as they have been concerned with the substance of bargaining, they have been negative (for example, a policy of resisting demands for a union shop or for promotion exclusively by seniority). In this connection the distinguishing feature of the formula wage policy is that it represents a positive long-term policy involving the substance of bargaining.

It is this concern with the substance or content of collective bargaining that justifies making an extended analysis and evaluation of the formula system and its variants. The practice of combining wage-price adjustments with escalator clauses and annual increases has been followed by employers in other major industries, such as steel, aluminum, railroads, meat packing, and electrical equipment. Even more important, however, the GM-UAW contracts have probably contributed more than any other single factor to the acceptance of annual wage increases as part of the American wage earner's way of life. A good case can be made for the argument that the philosophy of the wage formula—that money wages should be regularly increased both to offset price increases and to provide for a higher living standard—acquired the status of an informal national wage policy during the 1950's.[29] The current assumption that annual wage increases are part of an immutable pattern of industrial relations rests on a number of bases, but no one of them is more directly responsible for its acceptance than the 1948 GM-UAW contract, its successors and imitators.

[29] In this study "national wage policy" is not intended to refer to an explicit set of criteria to be implemented by a national wage board. The usage here is meant to suggest an informal consensus about appropriate wage policy that appears to guide the decisions of a major part of the national economy.

3

Wage Policy and the Feasible Rate of Wage Increase

EARLIER IT WAS noted that the combination of the escalator clause and the annual improvement factor in the wage formula focused attention on perhaps the most critical question involved in devising a wage formula or in promulgating a general wage policy: What rate of increase in real wages is appropriate for wage policy? This chapter tries to answer that question.

The problem of the appropriate rate of real wage change is found in all economies, regardless of the form of economic organization or the method of setting wages. The issue is particularly relevant in the context of the wage formula because its official rationale is based on the proposition that the real wages of specific groups ought to rise at a rate equal to the increase in productivity for the economy as a whole —not for General Motors, the automobile industry, or any other particular sector. The question arises whether, even within these partial segments of the economy, the programmed rate of wage increase is appropriate to accomplish the objectives of the policy makers.

A broader question is raised if the formula is viewed as being applicable to industry as a whole. The next two chapters evaluate the formula technique as a model for wage policy to be applied to a major section, if not the great bulk, of the private economy. Most of the discussion and criticism of the formula approach has been concerned with the consequences that might be expected to follow from its adoption over broad areas of the economy.[1] In the opinion of the writer, the

[1] For one of the more complete discussions of the escalator and productivity factors see Jules Backman, *Wage Determination* (Van Nostrand, 1959). See also the symposium on the implications of the formula contracts for the economy as a whole in the *Review of Economics and Statistics* (November 1949).

great interest attracted by this innovation resulted, not from its potential effect on General Motors or the automobile industry, but from
the problems that might be posed by its widespread acceptance
throughout the economy.

The casual follower of the public discussion of wage-price relationships so common during the postwar period may be surprised that an
extended analysis of the relation between wages and productivity is
necessary. Statements that "wage increases that do not exceed gains in
productivity are not inflationary" are commonplace and, moreover, are
essentially true. Unfortunately, they are ambiguous and are particularly untrustworthy when applied to particular collective bargaining
situations. This chapter and the next try to make them somewhat more
precise and to indicate some of the problems involved in moving from
a comfortable level of generality to the sticky issues of specific policy
decisions.

The Feasible Rate of Wage Increase

The key concept in this chapter is "the feasible rate of wage increase," defined initially as the annual rate of increase in hourly wage
rates compatible with a stable price level and the existing functional
distribution of income.[2] (Interpret all rates as compounded annually.)

Alternative Ways of Raising Real Wages

The wage formula presupposes a continuing increase in real wages
and provides for distributing this increase by raising money wages with
average consumer prices stable. Since real wages are defined as money
wages corrected for changes in prices, the wage-price relationship built
into the formula is only one of a number of ways in which real wages

---

[2] "Functional distribution of income" refers to the division of income according to
the economic "functions" being rewarded. For example, wages and salaries are paid
for labor services, interest for the use of money capital, and so on. An actual rate
of wage increase higher than the feasible rate may not cause inflation if it is accompanied by offsetting changes in the prices per unit of the other factors of production, changes in the functional distribution of income or a combination of these.

can be raised. Put in their simplest form, the alternatives are: (a) to increase money wages with average prices stable or (b) to decrease prices with average wages held stable.

Choosing between these two involves dealing with some of the most subtle and controversial questions of economic analysis. It is impossible in this study to do justice to this range of issues. For our purposes stable prices with rising wages (incomes) is adopted as the appropriate goal of policy for the following reasons: (1) Historically, productivity and wages have increased at least since 1899, and increases in real wages have been realized by raising money wages, although not necessarily at the feasible rate; (2) policy statements of the economic agencies of the government (for example, the Council of Economic Advisers and the Federal Reserve System) typically accept implicitly or explicitly, the goal of stable prices; (3) although no vote has ever been taken, in the writer's opinion, the economic literature indicates that the majority of the economics profession would choose this approach as a long-run policy.

It should be emphasized that distributing the fruits of productivity gains by raising wages does not imply that the recipients of the higher incomes are being rewarded for having themselves brought about the increase in productivity. If real wages were increased by decreasing prices, no one would assume that the direct beneficiaries of the lower prices had brought about the increase in productivity that made the lower prices possible. In this section, the question is one of the mechanics by which real wage increases are diffused through the economy.

The reader is further reminded that "stable prices" and "rising wages" refer to average behavior and are compatible with a rise, a fall, or stability in any particular wages and prices.

In part the basis for criticism of the wage formula is that changes in productivity are very difficult to measure statistically and that existing data are only approximations. More fundamentally, the objections are aimed at the failure to develop and apply the methodology of the formula wage policy precisely and unambiguously. (In a collective bargaining situation these analytical vices may on occasion prove to be eminently practical virtues.) The charge of imprecision is directed against not only the negotiators of wage formula contracts but also the academicians who have promulgated the doctrine of the noninflationary character of wage increases that are within the bounds of increases in productivity. So assiduously has this idea been advanced that it has been elevated to the status of a political platitude. In fairness to the economists, it should be pointed out that it is valid as long as it is interpreted in the proper context. Originally developed for pedagogical purposes in courses in elementary economics, the basic proposition is that as long as the wage per unit of labor does not increase so rapidly as to raise unit labor costs, the rise in wages will have no direct effect on prices. This is true virtually by definition, provided the economists involved are permitted to formulate the definitions.

Difficulties arise when the proposition is taken from the classroom to the bargaining table. In common usage, output per man-hour is considered to be a measure of productivity. In collective bargaining and in common speech, "wages" usually refers to the hourly wage rate. It is only natural that the statement should be interpreted to mean that increases in wage rates that do not exceed increases in output per man-hour are not inflationary.

The Income Approach and the Productivity Approach

Perhaps the best way to clarify the difficulties involved in translating the original generalized proposition about broad aggregates into a specific wage policy is that suggested by Lloyd Reynolds.[3]

In discussing the problem of defining a noninflationary wage policy, Reynolds distinguishes between the "income approach" and the "productivity approach." The objectives of the wage formula policy stated in Chapter 2 are consistent with the income approach. The implementation of these objectives through the wage formula typically relies on the productivity approach. The attempt to reach an objective that is at least implicitly stated in terms of annual per-capita income by changing hourly wage rates creates the special set of problems that are the burden of the criticisms noted in this section.

The actual amount of increase in real income of the population generated by economic progress is, of course, unaffected by the choice made between the income and the productivity approaches as tech-

---

[3] Lloyd G. Reynolds, "Wage Behavior and Inflation," in Charles E. Myers (ed.), *Wages, Prices, Profits and Productivity* (American Assembly, 1959), pp. 117-20.

niques of analysis. In the present state of the art of measuring real income and productivity, however, it would be surprising if the two approaches arrived at the same feasible rate of increase. The income approach is perhaps best for explaining the economic logic of the formula wage policy from the standpoint of the economy as a whole over the long run. Difficulties introduced by the changing rates of labor force participation and the changing distribution of workers among occupations and industries can be handled more easily in this context. On the other hand, the productivity approach has some real advantages for dealing with questions involving wage policy for particular industries or occupational groups. For expository purposes some problems common to both approaches will be discussed in terms of the income approach. The productivity approach will be used in the rest of the analysis because of its advantages in analyzing wage policy for specific sectors of the economy and for estimating the feasible rate of wage increase.

The Income Approach

Reynolds suggests that a first approximation to a noninflationary wage policy would call for wage income per capita to rise at the same rate as real national output per capita. This would of course allow non-wage income per capita to rise at the same rate without a direct impact on the price level. Under these circumstances the gains from increasing productivity would be distributed according to the pattern called for by the wage formula—through rising incomes including wages.[4]

It should be emphasized that the rate of increase in per capita output is not a measure of the maximum noninflationary rate of increase in wages nor of the rate of increase in productivity in the usually accepted sense. For example, it tells us nothing about the rate of in-

---

[4] Simon Kuznets estimates the rate of increase in real output per capita in "Quantitative Aspects of the Economic Growth of Nations," *Economic Development and Cultural Change* (October 1956), p. 10. Kuznets reports an average rate of growth of 16.4 per cent per decade or 1.5 per cent per year over the years 1894-1954.

Raymond Goldsmith cites this estimate of an average growth rate of 1⅝ per cent per year in real GNP per head from 1839 to 1959 in a statement in *Employment, Growth, and Price Levels*, Hearings before the Joint Economic Committee, Pt. 2. Historical and Comparative Rates of Productivity and Prices, 86 Cong. 1 sess. (1959), pp. 235, 239.

crease in the wages of employed workers that would produce this rate of increase in real wage income per capita. Neither does it indicate the rate of increase in output per man-hour or per worker employed that would produce this increase in per capita real income. Converting the "per capita" figures of the income measure to the "per hour" equivalents of either the wage or the output per man-hour measures is a complex task.

The derivation of a numerical estimate of a feasible rate of wage increase will be handled by the productivity approach in a later section. At this point it will be helpful to use the income approach to try to clarify three issues that are a common source of confusion whatever the framework of analysis. *First,* in an economy in which advancing productivity permits a particular increase in average income per capita, what effect does reducing the number of hours worked (or paid for) per employee have on the relation between the observed increase in real output and the feasible rate of wage increase per hour? *Second,* since the average earnings of workers may be changed by shifts from one job to another without any change in the wage rates for the different jobs taking place, what effect has the changing occupational and industrial composition of the labor force had on the feasible rate of wage increase associated with the increase in real output achieved in the past? *Third,* since many nonwage items of compensation (that is, fringe benefits) increase real income just as direct wage increases do, how should these be taken into account in drawing up a noninflationary wage policy? These questions will be considered in turn.

1. Changes in the average number of hours worked or paid for per worker.

While real output per capita was increasing at a rate of about 1.5 per cent per year between 1894 and 1954, according to Kuznets, average hours worked per week were dropping from 60.2 in 1900 to 40.0 in 1955.[5] It is probable that average hours worked per year behaved in about the same fashion.

This means that in addition to the increases in goods and services included in the index of real output, the average worker gained a very

[5] J. F. Dewhurst and Associates, *America's Needs and Resources: A New Survey* (Twentieth Century Fund, New York, 1955). Appendix 20-4, p. 1073. It should be noted that this reduction is partly a result of changing patterns of industrial employment.

sizeable increase in leisure. The reduction in hours worked and paid for, however, implies that, if per capita income is to be increased at, say, 1.5 per cent per year, hourly wages must go up this amount plus an additional amount sufficient to offset the reduction in hours paid for. For the 50 or 60 year period under discussion this means that an increase in hourly wages of about 2.25 per cent per year would have been needed to raise per capita income 1.5 per cent. (Since the productivity approach compares output per man-hour with earnings per hour, adjustment for changing hours takes place automatically.)

Until after World War II there was probably little reason to distinguish between hours worked and hours paid for, at least as far as production workers were concerned. Since 1945, however, this distinction has become important for both wage and productivity measures, and its significance will probably continue to increase. For our purposes, the proper concept to use is hours paid for. A paid holiday or vacation-with-pay decreases the number of hours worked per year without changing the number of hours for which wages are paid. Under these circumstances, annual per capita income is maintained even though per capita hours actually worked decline. Obviously there is no reason to increase hourly wages to achieve a given level of real income because of the drop in hours worked in this case.

The distinction between hours worked and hours paid for is important to both the income and the productivity approaches. Data that are available for output per man-hour worked show a rate of increase of 3.5 per cent for the private economy during 1947-58. Using man hours paid for in the denominator reduces the rate to 3.1 per cent.[6] In general, analyses of the relation between hourly earnings and productivity should use one set of hours data consistently, preferably hours paid for.

2. The relationship between changes in the earnings of individuals and rates of pay of jobs as the composition of the labor force shifts.

Although wage formulas are implemented by changing the rates of pay for classes of jobs, the logic of the formula approach is couched in terms of the earnings of individuals. It is theoretically possible to increase per capita income or average hourly earnings an amount equal to increasing productivity without changing a single wage rate as workers shift from lower paying to higher paying jobs. If wage rates

[6] U.S. Bureau of Labor Statistics, *Trends in Output per Man-Hour in the Private Economy, 1909-1958*, Bulletin No. 1249 (1959), p. 7.

were also increased at the same time, a kind of double counting of productivity gains would occur.

The usual analysis of this situation assumes that there is a systematic tendency for employment in higher paid jobs and industries to expand relative to lower paid jobs. In other words, the earnings of individual workers are assumed to be rising more rapidly than the wage rates for individual jobs because of the movement of workers to higher paid jobs on balance. The most important single factor supporting this view in the past has been the obvious shift of manpower from low-paying agricultural jobs to the higher paying sectors of manufacturing, transportation, and so on.

A closer examination of this issue suggests that the assumption that earnings increase substantially faster than wage rates may not be as soundly based as is generally believed.

There is very little evidence available to test how average hourly earnings within individual companies behave compared with average changes in wage rates. A recent study of the relationship between earnings and rate changes by industry has been published by John Maher.[7] Maher found that over the period 1945-57 the trend in earnings and rates for individual industries frequently diverged substantially in both directions. When the data for the separate industries were combined in weighted indexes of earnings and rate changes, the patterns of change for the two measures were found to be remarkably similar.

Turning to the effect of the changing composition of employment on hourly earnings for the economy as a whole, there is some further evidence that much of the casual discussion exaggerates its impact. In connection with his study of labor force behavior, Clarence Long developed a comprehensive average hourly earnings series for the period 1940-56.[8] Two series were constructed; one in which the earnings by industry were weighted by the industrial distribution of employment in 1940 and another weighted by the 1956 distribution. This procedure permits measurement of the effects of shifts of employment among in-

[7] John E. Maher, "Wages: The Pattern of Wage Movements in the United States Since 1945—Its Meaning and Significance," *Review of Economics and Statistics* (August 1961), pp. 277-82.

[8] Clarence D. Long, *The Labor Force Under Changing Income and Employment* (Princeton University Press, 1958) pp. 365-66. The series cover manufacturing, mining, public utilities, trade, services, railroads, coal, government, and agriculture and includes salaried non-supervisory workers in railroads and all employees in government.

dustries on average earnings between these two years. The influence of such industry shifts was found to be negligible since over the 16-year period, the series with 1956 weights increased only 4 cents more than the series with 1940 weights ($1.91-$1.87). Solomon Fabricant also noted with some surprise that between 1889 and 1957 an index of average hourly earnings for wage earners in manufacturing increased at about the same rate as a rough index of average hourly earnings for all workers in the private economy, including proprietors and family workers. The broader the area of the economy covered by an index, the greater the opportunity for employment shifts to raise earnings relative to rates. On these grounds, one would have expected the all workers index to rise substantially faster than the manufacturing workers index since the former covers four to five times as many persons. Although the data are approximate, there is no evidence that this occurred.[9]

It is possible that the apparent failure of shifts in the occupational and industrial structure of employment to raise earnings relative to wage rates can be explained by an important long-run change in the labor force that is often neglected. Not only do workers shift among occupations and industries, but shifts into and out of the labor force itself are occurring. These changes affect the behavior of hourly earnings series just as do shifts among jobs by members of the existing labor force.

The most dramatic labor force development of the past half century has been the changing sex composition of the employed. Long reports that between 1890 and 1950 women workers rose from 17 to 27 per cent of the labor force.[10] One forecast is for a rise to 33 per cent by 1975.

This change in sex composition is the result of a secular rise in the labor force participation rate for women accompanied by a secular decline in participation rates for men. Since women, on the average, seem to have earned from one-half to two-thirds as much as men during the period covered by Long's data,[11] the shift in the sex composition of

---

[9] Solomon Fabricant, *Basic Facts on Productivity Change* (National Bureau of Economic Research, 1959), pp. 32-33.

[10] Long, *op. cit.*, pp. 285-86. The 1975 forecast is from U. S. Bureau of the Census, *Current Population Reports*, Series P-50, No. 42. Data are for the population 14 years of age and over.

[11] Long, the same, p. 356.

employment has acted to lower broad averages of earnings relative to the averages of rates of pay.

It is still probably true, particularly within individual companies, that average earnings tend to rise relative to average rates of pay. As the time period lengthens and the area of the economy under consideration broadens, this conclusion may not be valid, and the effect could conceivably be in the opposite direction.

As far as its relevance for wage policy is concerned, the net effect of shifts in the composition of the labor force is probably in the direction of higher earnings but, considering the economy as a whole or broad sectors of it, it is not at all clear that this factor is nearly as significant in raising earnings as is often assumed.

3. The growth in importance of nonwage benefits.

The growth in nonwage or fringe benefits as part of employee compensation is a matter of common knowledge. Over the period 1947-1957, the U. S. Chamber of Commerce reports that fringe benefits rose from 15 to 23.7 per cent of payroll in 102 identical companies.[12] These figures tend to overstate the magnitude of the payments in proportion to payroll since the Chamber uses a broad definition of "fringes" and because larger companies and companies with more elaborate programs are probably over-represented in the group responding to the questionnaire. The rate of growth illustrated by these figures is probably much more representative of the true situation than are the absolute amounts.

Critics of wage formulas have argued that the monetary value of these benefits should be considered part of "wages." If this were done, it would act to reduce the feasible rate of increase in *direct* wages associated with any particular increase in per capita output or productivity.

As a general principle, this contention is correct. Any claim on the goods and services that are included in the output figure used in calculating either productivity or per capita output per year is part of the "wage" of the individual concerned. This is true whether that claim is created by paying a direct money wage or by a supplementary payment or transfer of income.

[12] U. S. Chamber of Commerce, *Fringe Benefits 1957* (1959), p. 28.

The Productivity Approach

Although the income approach is, for some analytical purposes, preferable to the productivity approach because it makes explicit the role of factors such as changing labor force participation rates, shifts in occupational composition, and changing hours of work, both techniques were found to produce approximately the same feasible rate of wage increase. Because the language and the methodology of the productivity approach is more familiar to the average citizen and the average businessman or labor leader, it will be used for the remainder of the analysis.

The use of data on productivity change in discussing the economics of wage policy works from the side of the cost of production rather than per capita income. An increase in output per man-hour reduces the quantity of labor required per unit of product and permits an increase in the wage rate without increasing labor cost per unit. Unfortunately, the emphasis on the cost side has led in the past to the confusion of two different problems. In their simplest form, one of the problems is the normative or prescriptive question of formulating a desirable wage policy for the economy as a whole. The other issue is the question of the direct effect of a specific wage decision on unit labor costs and prices of a particular company. The distinction is between asking whether a wage change *should* have occurred and assessing the effects of one that has in fact occurred.

Until recent years, productivity data have been relatively difficult to come by. Although major conceptual and statistical problems still exist, current interest in wage, price, profit, and productivity relationships has stimulated a number of studies that have expanded and refined the data available so that the prospects of using productivity data in relatively rigorous analysis are more promising than they have been in the past. Formerly, most of the productivity studies were restricted to variations of one type of measure, output per man-hour, and to limited sectors of the economy. Under the spur of events, both the Bureau of Labor Statistics and private sources have improved the basic data available.[13]

[13] The work of John Kendrick particularly deserves mention in this connection. See his *Productivity Trends in the United States,* published for the National Bureau

Exclusive reliance on changes in output per man-hour in the analysis of wage changes ignored the fact that a change in unit labor cost is not the same thing as a change in the unit cost of production. A reduction in unit requirements of one type of labor or of all labor combined may be purchased at the cost of increasing the requirements of other factors in one form or another. Changes in output per man-hour do not measure the reduction in real costs of production when all resources used in production are taken into account. This is, of course, true particularly when the measure of labor requirements used is output per production worker man-hour. In recent years the expansion of indirect or nonproduction worker employment relative to production workers has made this problem particularly acute.[14]

By use of the new data from recent studies, some of these problems can be clarified. Table 1 reproduces several different measures of the long-term rate of increase in productivity in the United States. Depending on the measure used, the average annual rate for the private domestic economy varies from 2.3 to 1.0 per cent over the period 1889-1957. The highest figure results when total man-hours of all employees is used as the denominator of the output/input ratio. When the man-hours used in higher paid industries are given more weight than the man-hours in lower paid industries, the rate of increase is reduced to 2.0 per cent per year.[15]

During the periods covered by Table 1, the amount of capital used in production increased more rapidly than did the amount of labor. As a result, when the growth of output per unit of capital is measured, the rate falls to 1.0 per cent per year. When the two types of input are combined, output per unit of combined labor and capital rose at a rate of only 1.7 per cent annually. This latter figure is the best available

---

of Economic Research by the Princeton University Press, 1961. Some of Kendrick's results were released earlier in the publications cited in this chapter. The Bureau of Labor Statistics has expanded its excellent program in this area.

[14] See Charles L. Schultze, *Recent Inflation in the United States*, Study Paper No. 1, Study of Employment, Growth, and Price Levels, Joint Economic Committee (1959), pp. 84-90, and Ruth P. Mack, "Inflation and Quasi-Elective Changes in Costs," *Review of Economics and Statistics* (August 1959), pp. 225-31.

[15] This adjustment is based on the theory that differences in pay measure differences in "quality" of the man-hours involved. Quality is seen as a function of skill, education, and experience, and the use of a given number of higher quality hours is treated as equivalent to the use of a larger number of lower quality hours. Insofar as differences in pay do not reflect differences in quality in this sense but are the result of differences in effort expended, differences in the attractiveness of the job, or differences in institutional factors (for example, unionism), this procedure may be questioned.

TABLE 1. *Average Annual Percentage Rates of Change in Measures of the Increases in Productivity and Wages*

	1889–1957	1919–57	1948–57
(1) Real product per unit of:			
Total factor input..............	1.7	2.1	2.1
Capital input...................	1.0	1.3	−.02
Weighted man-hours............	2.0	2.4	3.1
Unweighted man-hours..........	2.3	2.6	3.4
(2) Total real compensation per			
man-hour, manufacturing........	2.4	2.8	3.5
		1909–57	
(3) Real product per man-hour:			
Total, private economy...........		2.2	3.2
Manufacturing.................		n.a.	2.7
(4) Total real compensation per			
man-hour, manufacturing.........		2.9	3.5
(Average annual rates computed by compound interest formula.)			

Sources: (1) John Kendrick, "Productivity, Costs and Prices," in Charles E. Myers (ed.), *Wages, Prices, Profits and Productivity*, (American Assembly, 1959), Table 1, p. 43. Productivity data are for the private domestic economy. Man-hour data are primarily for hours worked.
(2) Albert Rees, "Patterns of Wages, Prices and Productivity," in Myers (ed.), the same, Table 1, pp. 15–16. Includes fringe costs and covers wage earners.
(3) U. S. Bureau of Labor Statistics, *Trends in Output per Man-Hour in the Private Economy, 1909–1958*, Bulletin No. 1249 (December 1959), Tables 1 and 5. Series used are based on man-hours paid for.
(4) Rees, "Patterns of Wages, Prices and Productivity," pp. 15–16.

measure of the decline in real costs of production per unit of output, or put differently, it is a measure of the gains available for distribution.

At first glance, it may seem that when the rate of change in output per unit of labor and capital combined is ascertained, the search for a feasible rate of wage increase would be at an end. Unfortunately, the issue is complicated by considerations of income distribution. Defining "wage income" as all payments (including salaries) for labor services wherever performed and "property income" as all nonwage income, permits us to develop the following tentative statements about the relationship between wage changes and income shares:[16]

[16] "Tentative" because, in some instances, they do not take into account factor substitution as relative prices and technological possibilities change. The assumption of stable income shares usually made in discussions of wage policy is a crucial one and, in a sense, avoids what may be the fundamental issue. Technological change almost certainly is either capital-using or capital-saving (that is, it increases or decreases capital requirements per unit of output) on balance in any time period. It would be surprising if this resulted in unchanged shares of income, but the discussion in the text can only suggest some of the implications of the simplest case.

1. If all rates per unit of labor services and all prices per unit of property were increased at a rate equal to that of the increase in combined productivity, the division of total real income between the wage and property shares would be directly related to the changes in the relative quantities of labor and of property used in production. Since the supply of property or capital has been increasing faster than the supply of labor, this would mean that property income would account for a progressively larger proportion of total income, other things remaining equal.

Leaving aside the question of equity, in view of the relative concentration of ownership of property, this situation might well be socially undesirable and politically unstable.[17] Proposals to deal with this problem by achieving a much more widespread distribution of property are laudable but, to date, of limited relevance.

If wage rate changes are geared to the index of combined productivity while other factor prices are left free to vary, the effect on income distribution is impossible to predict in any concrete situation. The marginal productivity theory of income distribution indicates that the result would depend on such influences as the relative rates of change in the quantities of labor and capital, and the rate and character of technological change. Rough generalizations based on average productivity changes are inadequate for venturing into this question although they are helpful in pointing up the issues.

2. In debates about wage policy (for example at the time of the 1959-60 steel dispute), it has been argued that when wage increases for production workers are under consideration, the appropriate measure of productivity change is output per man-hour of production workers. If production worker wage rates were changed in proportion to changes in the productivity of production workers, the income share of this group

[17] The use of "socially undesirable'" in this context has been challenged on the ground that, under certain assumptions, it would be possible for an increasing property share to be functionally responsible for a rate of increase in the absolute share of labor that would be greater than the rate of increase of labor income associated with a stable or declining share of property income. In other words, an increasing percentage of property income might result in nonproperty income being a relatively smaller but absolutely larger piece of a much larger pie. The use of socially undesirable in the text implies certain value judgments about the range of differentials in individual or family incomes as well as total income shares.

in a company, industry, or the national economy would be a constant percentage of total real income.[18]

3. In addition to the index of changes in combined productivity and indexes based on a single occupational group there are a sizable number of alternatives for consideration as standards for wage policy. Without examining each in detail, a promising candidate as a measure of the feasible rate of wage increase that would be noninflationary and relatively neutral in its effects on income distribution appears to be the index of output per man-hour paid for of all employees, broadly defined. Were all "wages" adjusted in proportion to changes in this index, the division of total real income between wage and property income would tend to be stable in percentage terms. If, as Kendrick's data suggest, the productivity of capital increases less rapidly than this measure, the result would be a tendency for the price per unit of capital or property to decline relative to wages.[19]

At this point the reader needs to be warned that this brief review of the effect of these different approaches to wage determination on shares of income is not meant to imply that wage policy is the dominant influence on trends in income distribution. Probably most economists would agree that the tax and expenditure policies of government are more effective mechanisms for changing the pattern of income distribution than is wage policy. In the opinion of the writer, however, it is possible for a wage policy to influence the distribution of income among the various occupational groups in the population and also between wage and property income for substantial periods of time. The

[18] For an oversimplified illustration of this point: assume an increase in output per production worker man-hour that expresses itself as a 10 per cent decrease in man-hours needed to produce a constant level of output. If wage rates per hour are increased 10 per cent, total payroll would remain constant and, *ceteris paribus*, would remain the same percentage of total income.

[19] The concept of the "price per unit" of capital was developed by Kendrick to meet the problem raised because the "rate of return" on capital is not analogous to the wage rate as the price of labor. Wage rates are absolute dollar magnitudes related to an unchanging time unit. The rate of return is a percentage concept and introduces problems of the valuation of the capital base. The price per unit of capital takes account of changes in the rate of return and in the prices of capital goods. See John W. Kendrick, "Trends in Product Prices, Factor Prices and Productivity," *Compendium: The Relation of Prices to Economic Stability and Growth*, Joint Economic Committee (1958), pp. 225-35.

range of potential variation is probably not wide, but neither is it inconsequential. This is particularly likely to be true if the wage policy in question is one widely accepted as socially desirable, such as the principle of "solidarity" in vogue in some of the countries of northern and western Europe in the postwar period.

Historical Wage Trends and the Feasible Rate

Two of the productivity indexes seem particularly relevant to the problem of choosing a feasible rate of wage increase; Kendrick's index of real product per unit of labor and capital combined and a series of real product per man-hour of all employees. In recent years the Bureau of Labor Statistics has produced a measure of productivity change that is a close approximation to the latter index. It is an index of real product per man-hour paid for of all persons employed, including proprietors and unpaid family workers. Data from this series are included in Table 1. Unfortunately, as the table indicates, the two series not only show different levels of productivity increase, but the difference between them has been increasing. The Kendrick combined factor index probably represents the lower limit while the Bureau of Labor Statistics series is the upper limit. Although the issue cannot be regarded as closed, the emphasis on income shares in the definition of the feasible rate suggests that the BLS series is a closer approximation to that hypothetical rate.

If the index of output per man-hour for all employees is accepted as the best available measure of the feasible rate of wage increase, how do the scheduled wage changes of the formula and actual wage changes compare with this standard?

Over the half century, 1909-57, this measure of real product per man-hour increased at an average annual rate of 2.2 per cent. For recent time periods, productivity measures typically show a higher rate of increase. For this series, real product per man-hour increased at 3.2 per cent per year from 1948 through 1957.

These data suggest that the GM-UAW annual improvement factor of 2.5 per cent per year in direct wages is somewhat above the long-run feasible rate of wage increase but, even when the cost of fringes is added, may not be far from the feasible rate characteristic of the postwar period. In Chapter 5, however, some evidence is presented that in actual practice real average hourly earnings (not wage rates) in the motor vehicle industry have increased at a 3-per-cent rate during this period, with the rate rising to 4 per cent with a conservative estimate of fringe costs included. In some of the other industries using formula-type contracts the annual growth in direct increases excluding fringes ranged upward from 3 to almost 4 per cent in the fifties.

In the original version of the formula contracts, it appears that the scheduled increases in real wages were within the general bounds of the feasible rate, but as these contracts worked out in practice, increases in earnings may have exceeded these limits to some extent. Some of the pattern followers in other industries seem to have been clearly outside the feasible rate range.

Both in this chapter and, in greater detail, in the next chapter, however, we have argued that the relevant comparison is between the feasible rate and the rate of change for "wages" over the economy as a whole and not individual industries. Unfortunately, there is no average wage figure for the economy as a whole. If Rees' data on total real compensation per hour in manufacturing (Table 1) is acceptable as a substitute, the actual rate of wage change has been substantially higher than the hypothetical feasible rate for 1909-57 as a whole. For the 1948-57 period, the discrepancy shrinks to less than 10 per cent.

If real wages have gone up faster than the rate compatible with stable prices and stable income shares, one or the other or both of these conditions must have been violated. In the writer's opinion, the evidence suggests that at one time period or another, one or both developments have occurred.[20]

To sum up: The feasible rate of wage increase, defined as the rate compatible with price stability and an unchanged functional distribution of income, appears to have been in the neighborhood of 2-2.25 per cent per year over the past 50-75 years. This range of values is produced by both the income and productivity approaches. The output per man-hour indexes of the productivity approach suggest that the feasible rate has been rising and that in the postwar period it has been in the

[20] This implies that the property share of national income has decreased over time. In recent years this view has been more widely accepted. Kendrick reported a decline in capital's income share in the Joint Economic Committee, *Compendium, op. cit.,* pp. 225-26. His data show a drop from 28 to 21 per cent between 1919 and 1953.

neighborhood of 3.0 per cent (including fringe costs). This increase is not confirmed by the index of output per unit of combined input. Although the evidence is not conclusive, it appears that for the period as a whole real wages have actually risen at a rate in excess of the feasible rate. For the postwar years, the difference has been substantially less than for the period as a whole because of acceleration in the rate of productivity increase.

Relaxation of the condition that income shares be unchanged would permit a somewhat higher rate of increase in wages without inflation, but, for reasons discussed in Chapter 4, this tactic can provide only a temporary respite in a private enterprise economy.

In closing, it should be stressed again that the feasible rate of increase in real wages can be achieved either through stable prices and rising incomes or stable incomes with falling prices. Even if it is agreed that the rising income technique is preferable, the inevitable imprecision of the analysis suggests that a conservative approach is in order. However determined, the feasible rate should be regarded as the outside limit for a policy of raising wages. An underestimation of the feasible rate still leaves the falling price route to raising real wages available. The consequences of overestimation are likely to be more serious. As a final qualification, even if a feasible rate could be determined precisely, this would provide no guide to an appropriate settlement in individual wage negotiations, but would be applicable only to the economy as a whole.

A NOTE ON FRINGE BENEFITS

The problem of handling fringe benefits in wage-productivity analyses is one which is difficult to solve in a completely satisfactory fashion. The distinction between the income and the productivity approach can be helpful in illuminating the problem.

As noted in the section on the income approach, the cost of most fringe benefits should be included as part of "wages" in arriving at an estimate of the feasible rate of wage increase. The general principle proposed was that ". . . any claim on the goods and services that are included in the output figure used in calculating per capita per year is part of the 'wage' of the individual concerned."

When the more common productivity approach is used, the question becomes more complicated. When comparing changes in productivity and changes in wages most discussion has assumed that, in this context, the wage figure should include increases in fringe costs as well as direct wage increases. In spite of its surface plausibility, this conclusion is not obvious and may not be valid.

This can be seen by interpreting changes in productivity to mean something like Kendrick's output per unit of total factor input. It can be shown that the total outlay on each and every type of cost element (including profits and taxes) incurred in the operation of a business can increase at a percentage rate equal to the increase in productivity for the business.

As a simple arithmetic example, assume all costs are divided into capital and labor costs so that every $1.00 of output requires an outlay of 50 cents for each factor. Then if, as a result of an increase in productivity, the same quantities of capital and labor could produce $1.10 worth of output (a 10 per cent increase), the return to each claimant could rise to 55 cents (again, a 10 per cent increase).

This suggests that direct wage costs could increase at a rate equal to increases in productivity and, since fringes can be considered a distinct and separate claim on the company, they can also increase at the same rate as all other claims. This analysis is sometimes viewed as proving that it is not correct to add increases in fringe costs to increases in direct wages and compare the total to productivity changes. If the percentage increase in fringe costs is simply added to the percentage increase in direct wages and the comparison made, this procedure is indeed invalid. For example, assume in the illustration in the last paragraph that for each $1.00 of output, direct labor costs were $.45, fringe costs $.10, and capital costs $.45. Once again, a 10 per cent increase in combined factor productivity would permit a 10 per cent increase in the return to each factor. It would be wrong to add the cents-an-hour amounts represented by the 10 per cent increases in fringe costs and direct labor costs, express this amount as a percentage of direct labor costs, and compare the result to the 10 per cent increase in productivity.

It would be perfectly legitimate, however, to add together the direct labor and the fringe costs in cents for each period and compare the rate of increase for the combination to the rate of productivity increase. This is the procedure used in this study.

4

The Formula Approach
and Its Critics

MOST OF THE important criticisms of the formula approach are linked to one or the other of three major themes. (1) A system of wage adjustment that includes only changes in consumer prices and long-run average increases in productivity for the economy as a whole ignores other variables that are important in wage determination if the wage structure is to have the flexibility required in a changing, growing economy. (2) Even if a workable wage policy could be specified in detail, its implementation would be impossible in a context of "free collective bargaining" with aggressive and competitive unionism. (3) Even if these problems could be solved, wage formulas produce "built-in-inflation" in the sense that they provide a mechanism in which wage increases may lead to price increases that, through the escalator clause, set off new wage increases, thereby touching off a new cycle. This chapter takes up each of these criticisms in turn. Whereas the preceding chapter was concerned with estimating the feasible rate of increase in the wage level, this chapter deals with problems of achieving that average rate in the setting provided by the economic forces and institutions operating in the American decentralized bargaining system.

What Pattern of Wage Changes?

In its pure form the wage-formula version of the productivity wage policy implies a uniform annual rate of increase in real wage rates that, over the long run, matches the average rate of increase in the productivity of the economy. From the beginning, the contrast between the uniformity of the prescribed wage changes and the diversity of actual experience with changes in productivity has been pointed out by critics of the system. The logic of the wage formula calls for uniformity in the annual increase in real wages scheduled from year to year and, strictly interpreted, for uniform increases in wages throughout an industry and across industry lines throughout at least a major part of the economy.

The variability of changes in productivity as measured by the most commonly used index (output per man-hour) is easy to demonstrate whether attention is centered on changes over successive time periods or among various industries during the same time period.[1] Although no official data exist for individual companies, it is assumed that the companies within an industry typically show comparable diversity in performance.

On a formal level there is no difficulty in reconciling uniform wage changes with diversity of changes in productivity in a way consistent with a price level that displays long-run stability. As long as the rate of increase in real wages matches the average increase in productivity for the sector of the economy to which the wage formula is being applied, price inflation can, at least in theory, be avoided. Prices may fluctuate from year to year, from company to company, or from industry to industry, but it is logically possible for the various patterns of individual changes to average out so as to achieve price stability.

It is helpful to view the principal alternative methods of relating wages and productivity changes as being located on a continuum. At one extreme would be the method of adjusting the wage rate for each individual job to reflect the productivity increases on that job. Aside from practical considerations of measurement and application, this would be unworkable because of the tremendous range of changes in productivity that can be expected to occur over time among individual jobs. These changes are unlikely to be related to the performance of the specific worker on the job or to the factors (such as skill) that are usually accepted as bases for differences in wages. If job rates were tied directly to changes in productivity on individual jobs, the result would be a chaotic wage structure impossible to administer.

At the other extreme of the continuum would be the policy of mak-

---

[1] See, for example, Solomon Fabricant, *Basic Facts on Productivity Change* (National Bureau of Economic Research, 1959), pp. 42-47.

ing uniform changes in all wage rates equal to the appropriate rate of change in productivity. This would freeze the structure of wages existing at the time the system was introduced and would also be unworkable. As noted in later sections, the wage structure serves a number of purposes, including that of allocating the labor supply. It is unlikely that any given structure could perform this function without being able to adjust to changes in demand and supply.

Between these extremes lies a variety of approaches involving differential rates of change of wage rates for various sets or collections of jobs. Differential changes could be based on occupational classifications and related to varying rates of change in productivity by occupation. Alternatively, wage and productivity relationships could be placed on a company-by-company or an industry-by-industry basis. In the next section suggestions for relating wage and productivity changes by occupational groupings and by industry groupings are considered briefly. Whatever method of relating wage changes to productivity changes is adopted, as long as the average rates of change are equivalent, the arrangement could be noninflationary in principle.

It is not a valid criticism of this approach to argue that because productivity changes vary from company to company or from year to year, prices in companies or in years with below-average records may have to be raised. In theory, as long as the requirement that long-run average changes should be equivalent is met, these increases could be offset by decreases in companies and years with above-average increases.

On occasion both the opponents and the proponents of the formula approach have shown a curious lack of consistency in assessing the probability that this mechanism will actually produce a stable price level under these circumstances. Some analysts who are confident that price competition is vigorous enough to insure lower prices for consumers if only producers did not pre-empt all gains in productivity, doubt that price competition is strong enough to produce selective price declines in years and in companies with unusually high gains in efficiency. Similarly, economists who stress monopoly elements in price setting when discussing whether gains in real income should be distributed through lower prices or higher incomes, tend to become more optimistic in discussing the likelihood of selective price decreases in years and in companies with above-average gains in productivity. Unfortunately, the pessimistic conclusions of both groups may be justified. In recent years some economists have described price and wage behavior as exhibiting a "ratchet" effect, in which increases once established have turned out to be insensitive to downward pressures.

Insofar as this condition exists, it might be argued that the appropriate system of wage adjustment is one that minimizes the occasions for price increases. It would then become a question of fact as to whether a collective bargaining system that uses the wage-formula approach or one that relies on *ad hoc* annual bargaining with other sets of wage-determining factors triggers the greater number of price increases. While no conclusions are justified at this point, it is possible that the wage-formula system may be somewhat more likely to produce selective price increases because its mechanistic character tends to insulate it from the influence of the special circumstances surrounding individual bargains.

An important variant of this criticism stresses that the system of wage rates in the economy is subject to a variety of influences and is expected to perform a number of functions. If all of the existing "wage slack" that is generated by increases in productivity is distributed among the various claimants, other types of adjustment are precluded unless the limits of wage increases set by increases in efficiency are to be exceeded.

At any time the structure of wages performs several functions, two of which are the most important. From one standpoint the payment of wages distributes income generated in production, thereby providing consumers with money to buy the products of their labor and in the process determining their standard of living. From another standpoint the structure of wages for different types of labor acts to adjust demand and supply by allocating the available labor among competing uses and by encouraging the adjustment of supply to a constantly changing pattern of demand and vice versa. In its simple form, the wage formula concentrates on the income-generating aspect of wages and ignores the allocation function of wage differentials. Strictly applied, this approach would freeze wage relationships as they existed at the time of its introduction. If changes in relative wages for different skills are required to adjust to a new pattern of demand for labor, the wage increases involved would have to be in addition to the increases called for by the productivity wage policy system and hence would create an inflationary potential.

Possible Solutions

Assume that the system of changing individual wage rates to correspond with changes in productivity in individual jobs as well as that of changing all wages uniformly in correspondence with economy-wide changes in productivity are both unworkable, at least in the long run. This suggests the possibility of developing a wage policy tied to economic sectors of a scope intermediate between the extremes of individual jobs and all jobs considered as a unit. Three obvious possibilities suggest themselves. Wage policy might focus on wage adjustments by occupation, by company, or by industry. At first glance the company would appear to be the logical choice. Further reflection suggests, however, that a better case can be made for the "industry" (however defined) as the key element in wage movements. Union wage policy is typically industry oriented, and industry-wide (sometimes multi-industry) patterns seem to have been characteristic of the experience of the past quarter century. Economic theorizing about wages is couched in terms of the demand for, and supply of, homogeneous classes of labor and is therefore occupationally oriented. There have been attempts to approach the question of appropriate wage behavior on the basis of industry and occupation singly and in combination.

In Chapter 2 it was pointed out that at least two economists had suggested something like the GM-UAW annual improvement factor as a basis for wage policy in the years preceding the adoption of that policy. Professors Lerner and Hansen not only suggested that average wages should be related to the secular changes in average productivity, but recognized the difficulties involved in uniform changes or in changes unrelated to other influences. Each proposed a system of differential movements.[2]

Starting from the premise that the over-all rates of change of wages and productivity should correspond, Lerner suggested that the supply and demand conditions in various labor markets be made the basis for differential increases in wages. In areas and industries with a level of unemployment more than twice the national average, there would be no increases in wages or, at most, only increases well below the average

[2] Abba P. Lerner, "Money as a Creature of the State," *American Economic Review* (May 1947), pp. 312-17. Alvin H. Hansen, *Economic Policy and Full Employment* (McGraw-Hill, 1947), p. 247.

increase for the economy as a whole. In labor markets with less than half the national average rate of unemployment, wage increases greater than the national average would be permitted. This system would require massive changes in American economic philosophy and institutions, and, in spite of Lerner's persistence in advocating this idea, it is hard to regard it as a serious practical proposal.

The advantage of Lerner's concept is that it focuses attention on one of the most important reasons for differential wage changes—the need for adjusting wage policy to supply and demand conditions in labor markets. Although Lerner speaks in terms of "areas and industries," implicit in his argument is the possibility that differential wage changes among different types of labor, i.e., among different occupations in the same area or industry, might also be required on the same grounds.

Hansen's suggestions are less revolutionary in their implications. Starting from the fact that industries vary considerably in their rate of increase in output per man-hour, he advocates larger-than-average increases in wages in industries with larger-than-average increases in productivity and smaller-than-average increases in less technologically progressive industries. (In neither case is there to be exact correspondence between wage and productivity changes.) Hansen did not fully elaborate his wage policy since his main concern was with the conditions for price stability, but Dunlop carried this analysis one step further to tie it into labor market conditions.[3] Arguing that industries in which productivity was increasing most rapidly would be those that were also expanding employment, Dunlop held that the need to recruit more workers for these expanding industries would automatically lead to a correlation between increases in wages and increases in productivity.

The Hansen-Dunlop model has the advantage of generating differential wage changes that meet at least some of the requirements of the labor market without being inflationary and without relying on comprehensive controls. Unfortunately, the correlation between increases in productivity by industry and increases in employment seems to be rather low.[4]

[3] John T. Dunlop, *Income, Employment and Public Policy* (W. W. Norton, 1948), pp. 346-48.
[4] Fabricant, for example, reports a rank correlation coefficient of .34 between changes in productivity and changes in employment between 1899 and 1953. *Basic Facts on Productivity Change*, p. 29.

In spite of this, the possibility that differential annual increases in wages might simultaneously satisfy the criteria of price stability and the needs of the labor market should be considered. Other wage-determining factors, such as ability to pay, the will of management to resist, and the strength and aggressiveness of labor organizations, may reinforce the correlation between productivity and employment so that the combination of forces operating on wage decisions may produce workable results. Before it is concluded that wage formulas have introduced major elements of rigidity into the economy's mechanism for allocating labor, it should be remembered that the alternative to long-term contracts with formula-type adjustments is not the unorganized labor market but the highly organized markets of the past twenty years. With or without formulas, collective bargaining has in the past produced settlements that have been uniform throughout an industry and often across industry lines as well. There is a real question as to whether the formula approach, as it has actually worked in practice, has made wage settlements in any given year more uniform than they would have been otherwise. Wage formulas have probably made year-to-year increases more uniform than annual bargaining would have, but this may not be entirely undesirable.

Over more than two decades of collective bargaining, the tendency toward uniform settlements in diverse situations has not impeded the operations of the labor market in any obvious way. This may have been because the complex of forces affecting individual settlements have produced a pattern of wage behavior not far out of line with the requirements of labor allocation. This result may have been purchased at the cost of inflationary wage adjustments in at least some instances, and the formula approach may be open to the same criticism. In its defense, however, let it be pointed out that the formalization of the system has focused the debate and brought the problem forcibly to the attention of decision makers in all the organizations involved.

Finally, an unplanned wage policy may have proved viable because economists may have over-emphasized the importance of wage differentials as a means of allocating labor.[5] In the highly structured "institutional" labor markets of a modern industrial society, the existence of job opportunities and the interlocking and overlapping sets of rules governing access to jobs and defining the conditions of promotion,

---

[5] Economist Kenneth Boulding once remarked in speaking of his colleagues, "The market is our baby, and we can't help loving it a little."

transfer, layoff, and separation are undoubtedly more important for the operation of the labor market than the simple market model of classical economics would suggest. Researchers into the characteristics of labor mobility and into the "human relations" aspects of the work place have both questioned the primacy of economic motivation. Without question, in the long run wage differentials are an important influence in the allocation process, but when wages are high in absolute terms, when relative changes occur slowly, and when the responses of workers and managers are channeled through a "web of rules," workable wage behavior may encompass a wide range of alternative wage structures over relatively long periods of time.

These qualifications, however, do not invalidate the central point of the uniformity criticism. If formula-type adjustments are designed so as to exhaust the available wage gain, it is very likely that some extramural upward adjustments will occur somewhere in the system with a resulting cost pressure. In other words, the wage-formula approach to wage determination encourages the policy makers to exhaust all available wage slack by wage adjustments geared to only two of a larger set of wage-determining variables. In at least some other cases, other pressures for wage increases are certain to become operative with a resulting upward pressure on labor costs that could lead to some degree of price inflation.[6]

A Digression: The Wage Formula and Wage Incentives

A sizeable minority of American workers are paid according to some form of incentive system, and in some industries a majority of production workers are "on incentive." According to the BLS, about 27 per cent of all production workers in manufacturing in 1958 were paid on an incentive basis while the figure for the basic steel industry was 60 per cent.[7] The wage-formula approach to general wage changes presents some special problems under these circumstances.

[6] Professor Rees has pointed out that this assumes that "extra-mural" adjustments on balance will be in the upward direction. While downward adjustments might predominate, the possibility would not seem to be equally likely in the general case.

[7] L. Earl Lewis, "Extent of Incentive Pay in Manufacturing," *Monthly Labor Review* (May 1960), p. 461.

When the earnings of individuals or groups of workers are related to their output, two different problems arise. The first of these grows out of the tendency for workers on incentive pay systems to experience an upward "drift" or "creep" in their earnings over time. This may be due to the operation of a large number of factors, each of which singly appears to have a negligible effect but whose cumulative impact may be of some consequence. Workers may acquire more skill and dexterity, short cuts may be found, small changes in processes or adjustments in machinery may occur, improvements in lighting, materials handling, or other working conditions may be made, etc. When changes in conditions can be expected to have a consequential effect on earnings, the principles of wage administration call for a revision of production standards. In many instances, however, even alert and resourceful administrators find it impossible to control the situation completely. Insofar as a creep in earnings takes place, increases in productivity are being compensated for directly without any change in base rates. If a general increase in base rates is then awarded according to some version of the wage formula, a form of "double counting" of productivity increases takes place.

The second problem created by wage incentive systems is that most such plans are designed around a concept of a base rate, which establishes a minimum wage for an hour's work that is related to a given level of output as a production standard. Workers are given an incentive to produce above this standard by being paid an amount above the base rate geared to the degree by which the standard is exceeded. To be effective, an incentive system must be designed so that most workers will be producing above standard most of the time in order that there be a direct connection between their marginal effort and their marginal earnings. This is a possible source of another kind of double counting of productivity increases since the installation of a new incentive plan usually results in an increase of output per man-hour worked that is immediately and directly compensated for in the pay system without any necessary change in base rates.

In addition to this initial impact, the fact that actual hourly earnings are a multiple (say 1.2) of the base rate on the average means that any increase in base rates (in cents per hour), including those written into a wage formula, increases earnings by the appropriate multiple. For example, an increase of 10 cents an hour in base rates will increase the hourly earnings of the workers and the hourly wage cost of the company 12 cents under the conditions cited above. (The reader should note that the percentage change in wage rates and earnings will be the same.) One important by-product of this point is that two wage settlements providing nominally the same rate increase in cents per hour may have substantially different earnings and cost results in companies with different wage payment systems. The differing earnings experiences (noted in Chapter 5) of the steel and automobile industries under outwardly similar formula-type contracts are related partly to this issue.

Another important point to be noted is that the conversion into percentage terms of an average increase in cents per hour in base rates requires that it be related to average wage rates rather than to average hourly earnings. To illustrate, a 10-cents-an-hour increase in all base rates in a company with average hourly earnings of $2.50 need not mean that "wages" have been increased 4 per cent. If all workers are on incentive and are averaging 120 per cent of base rates, the true average increase in "wages" would be almost 5 per cent.[8]

It is important, therefore, to note that caution is required in drawing conclusions about the effects of reported wage settlements on costs and earnings. These effects are relevant whether a wage increase is negotiated on an *ad hoc* basis or is part of a formula settlement. But if the formula is intended to be related to changes in productivity, the special characteristics of incentive pay systems need to be taken into account.

Wage Policy and the Politics of Unionism

In an apt phrase, Arthur Ross has described the trade union as a "political agency operating in an economic environment."[9] It has become increasingly common to analyze the internal functioning of virtu-

[8] Depending on whether "wages" is interpreted as hourly earnings or as hourly rates, this calculation can be made by either (1) converting the 10-cent rate increase into the equivalent 12-cent earnings increase and expressing the latter as a percentage of earnings of $2.50, or (2) converting the $2.50 earnings figure into the appropriate average hourly rate (2.50 ÷ 1.2) and expressing the 10-cent rate increase as a percentage of the result.

[9] Arthur M. Ross, *Trade Union Wage Policy* (University of California Press, 1948), p. 12.

ally all economic organizations in similar terms, but the union is a political agency twice over as compared to, say, the business organization.
There is a "political" aspect to union functioning as the term is used
in analyzing any complex organization in which personal relationships
involve the use of authority, influence, and implicit bargaining. In addition, the union is a political institution in the formal sense of using
the apparatus of parliamentary democracy to select officers, decide policy, and ratify decisions.

There are two major reasons why the necessities of internal politics
of the union movement are alleged to make the orderly operation of a
general wage formula approach impossible. One of these grows out of
the relationships between the leaders and the rank and file of individual unions. The other relies on the existence of competition among
various unions, competition that takes the form of one union's attempting to match or surpass the wage settlements of its rivals.

As far as intra-union affairs are concerned, the critics' position is
that a "mechanical formula" for adjusting wages deprives the union of
an opportunity to demonstrate its value to the members at regular intervals. They claim that to retain the loyalty of its members the union must
periodically wring from a reluctant management concessions that
would not otherwise have been forthcoming. Whatever the programmed wage adjustments under formulas, their routine character
makes them unsuitable for their proper role in the drama of labor-management relations.

There are really two different problems involved in this situation.
One is the need for the union as an institution to attract continuously
the loyalty and support of at least a majority of the employees in the
bargaining unit. The development of "union security" arrangements in
a formal agreement between union and management that membership
will be compulsory as a condition of employment acts to reduce but
not eliminate the problem of institutional insecurity.[10] With compulsory membership provided by the union shop, the political apathy of
the membership can become something of an asset rather than a liability to the union leadership. Even if the employees remain convinced
of the value of the union as an organization, however, the problem of

---

[10] At the time of the signing of the five-year formula contract in 1950, General
Motors recognized the problem posed for the long-term security of the UAW by
the removal of the wage issue from bargaining and agreed to a form of the union
shop to protect the position of the union.

competition from rival candidates for leadership within the union remains. Typically, political rivalry of this sort takes the form of charges that the settlements being negotiated by the "ins" are not as advantageous as those that could be gained by more aggressive leadership. Even though the incumbents are protected by the bureaucratic inertia of large-scale organization, the tradition of strong constitutional protection of the prerogatives of leadership, and the availability of informal but effective techniques for dominating the internal political life of the union, they are not wholly immune from attacks of this type.

Not only are membership apathy and intra-union factionalism threats to institutional and leadership security, but inter-union rivalry presents still another potential threat to the existing order. In some cases the competition is direct, and one union may attempt to displace another as bargaining agent on the basis of relative ability to win favorable contracts. In other instances the accomplishments of the rival simply provide the yardstick against which the performance of the present office holders is measured and perhaps found wanting.

Traditionally, the union movement has tried to reduce competition among unions for members through the division of job territory into defined areas in each of which a single union is recognized as having exclusive jurisdiction, and by inter-union agreements to refrain from raiding already-established bargaining units. The effectiveness of these techniques in blunting the pressures which the combination of membership apathy and institutional and personal rivalry exert on union leaders to deliver something more than routinized results has varied over time, but they have never been entirely successful. To a greater or lesser degree, incumbent leadership in many unions feels a necessity to demonstrate its zeal in the pursuit of economic advantage over and above the gains provided automatically by wage formulas.

Undoubtedly the typical American union member requires a substantial show of strength at periodic intervals as the price of continued support of his bargaining representative. Concrete results that cannot be attributed to management beneficence are needed to convince him that the financial and other disabilities of membership are worthwhile. It is true that unionism provides very important nonmonetary benefits to its followers (for example, protection against arbitrary action by management). In the American environment, however, it is at least questionable whether these unspectacular achievements would hold worker allegiance if the acquisition of more tangible benefits became a matter of routine. Note that the United Automobile Workers' evaluation of the wage formula cited in Chapter 2 sees as a principal benefit of the system the assurance that the workers will maintain their relative position vis-à-vis other groups while being left "free to concentrate in their negotiations for a new agreement on the major objective of increasing their share in the total national product. . . ." There could then be considerable merit to the contention that, rather than determining the final settlement, the wage formula may simply provide a higher base from which the real bargaining begins. In Chapter 2 Charles E. Wilson was quoted as saying that the formula provided only the equivalent to the benefits that had resulted from conflict bargaining in the past. This view ignores the possibility that the constellation of forces that produced this result in the past may be fundamentally altered by the introduction of the formula philosophy as an explicit policy.

There is no doubt that there have been periods during which rival leadership in the union movement has created competition in winning wage gains, and this situation can pose a threat to the implementation of any wage policy.

The Wage Formula and Built-in Inflation

Although the charge has other aspects, the discussion of competitive unionism sets the stage for a consideration of the claim that wage formulas introduce a built-in or self-perpetuating inflationary bias into the economy.[11]

As a starting point, there is no question but that the formulas help maintain or intensify an inflationary movement that starts elsewhere in the economy. A price increase that originates anywhere in the domestic economy or that results from developments in international affairs sets off a rise in wage rates through the operation of the price escalator. If at all widespread, these cost increases are very likely to cause a secondary rise in prices, which leads to a second round of escalated wage increases, and the process is repeated. On the demand side, increases in wage earner income contribute to maintaining the process. The effects eventually become negligible after several "rounds," the length of

---

[11] Jules Backman reviews this issue in "Wage Escalation and Inflation," *Industrial and Labor Relations Review* (April 1960), pp. 398-410. Backman's discussion is confined to a consideration of the wage-price link alone.

time depending on the size of the initial impetus, the proportion of the income receivers included in the escalated sector, and the proportion escalated costs are of total costs.[12]

While there may be circumstances when the use of automatic formulas produces unfortunate social consequences, even in these instances the case against them sometimes rests on an oversimplified view of reality. Whatever its source, the burden of inflation is never distributed equally among all the economic interest groups in a society. Through a variety of institutional devices, both political and economic, the various groups try to minimize their portion of the burden. In the struggle to distribute the burden to their advantage, automatic adjustment of wages is a weapon in the arsenal of one important interest group—organized labor. It is not their only weapon. Political action in the areas of taxation, rationing, and subsidies and economic action through frequent wage bargaining are others. It is undoubtedly true that the formula approach reduces the lags in the adjustment process that are so important a part of any successful control mechanism, but the net effect from this factor alone is probably not large. The essence of the problem is that the power structure of the society influences the differential impact of inflation, and wage formulas are only one manifestation among many of the balance of economic power.

In the United States a second qualification to the usual indictment of the formula approach is important. The typical discussion of automatic wage adjustment and inflation implicitly assumes that there is a net burden in the form of an over-all reduction of living standards that has to be shouldered by society as a whole. Inflation is assumed to require such a reduction, and the policy problem is seen as that of apportioning this reduction in accordance with some standard of equity.

But in the United States during many years of rising prices there has been no "burden" in the usual sense to distribute. Between 1940 and 1960, a period including World War II and the Korean action, there were six years in which annual real per-capita disposable income fell below that of the previous year. In three of these six years the decline was less than 1 per cent ($12, $17, and $14), and the largest drop was approximately 6 per cent ($96).[13]

---

[12] It does not appear necessary for our purposes to discuss the possibility of monetary policy dampening this effect.

[13] The relevant data can be found in *1960 Supplement to Economic Indicators: Historical and Descriptive Background,* Prepared for the Joint Economic Committee by the Office of Statistical Standards, Bureau of the Budget, 86 Cong. 2 sess., p. 14. (The

Changes in real per-capita disposable income seems a logical measure of changes in average living standards since they include the effects of increasing population, changing prices, and changing taxes. It can be argued that the increases in income during World War II were illusory in that the price deflator (the CPI) did not reflect the impact of lower quality and goods shortages. During this period the burden of diverting goods from consumption to war uses (if any) was distributed through rationing procedures. Whatever allowance is made for these factors during these years, it would not change the main point made in the preceding paragraph.

Under these conditions some of the moral fervor goes out of attacks on protective devices. Slogans such as "fair shares for all" or "equality of sacrifice" carry more weight when the issue is one of apportioning a general reduction in living standards brought about by inexorable and impersonal economic forces. In the absence of such a general reduction, the situation appears as an extension of a continuing struggle for relative advantage in a dynamic economy, and the anti-formula argument loses some of its force.

In spite of these qualifications, however, there remains a possibly important class of situations in which cost-of-living escalation, alone or in combination with annual increases in the wage formula, can justly be charged with being a part of an "engine of inflation." It is true that the cost-of-living adjustment considered alone does not initiate inflation but, in the words of Charles E. Wilson ". . . simply adjusts the wages of our employees after the fact to what inflationary pressures have forced on the national economy. . . ." (See page 24.) When this adjustment is combined with annual wage increases or when it is considered as a part of a larger collective bargaining system characterized by aggressive unionism, however, the system as a whole may turn out to have a built-in inflationary bias.

The issue hinges on the magnitude of the annual wage increases called for by the improvement factor in the wage formula or produced by collective bargaining outside the area using the formula approach. If the annual increases in wages programmed in the wage formulas are

---

other two years showed drops of $37 and $32.) Some cautions concerning the use of such figures can be found in Albert Rees, "Patterns of Wages, Prices and Productivity," in Charles E. Myers (ed.), *Wages, Prices, Profits and Productivity* (American Assembly, 1959), pp. 18, 19.

such as to initiate a rise in the price index used for cost-of-living adjust-ments, then the two factors in combination constitute a built-in infla-tionary mechanism. The same situation arises if the annual increases under wage formulas are kept within noninflationary bounds, but the price index is raised by wage settlements negotiated outside the esca-lated sector. When the possibility of interunion competition between unions in the escalated and the nonescalated sector is introduced, the likelihood that a cumulative inflationary situation will develop is in-creased.

As usual, the picture is not all black. In the past, union-management interest in automatic cost-of-living adjustments has been most marked at times when prices were rising, or were expected to rise, fairly rap-idly. If automatic adjustments could not be arranged under these circumstances, negotiators would probably either (1) call for frequent reopenings of the wage issue, (2) attempt to forecast probable price increases over the duration of the contract and include at least a partial offset for them in the original settlement, or (3) provide for some com-bination of these two approaches. If the latter two strategies are at all widespread, the inflationary price anticipations tend to be self-realiz-ing. In this case, the cost-of-living escalators' contingent character makes it preferable to anticipatory increases since it permits the actual wage settlement to be reached without reference to potential inflation.[14] If the inflation fails to materialize, no wage adjustments occur. In the event of inflation, the adjustments occur after the fact, and their size is related directly to the actual price increases that have already occurred. In an economy as inflation-conscious as the American economy had be-come at the end of the 1950's, this is a major advantage.

Unfortunately, when formal cost-of-living adjustments cover part of the economy while other sectors bargain on an *ad hoc* basis, much of this advantage is lost. The very existence of the escalated agreements may increase the inflationary expectations of the nonescalated sector

---

[14] During inflationary periods, no increase, or only nominal increases, in industries that are relatively depressed are much easier to accept if the union is not forced to accept the risk of declines in real wages through price increases. Such a situation may have existed in textiles in some years of the fifties.

On the other hand, there seems little question that industries that appear to be reluctant to accept automatic wage-price links or even frequent reopenings (for example, contract construction) negotiated firm wage increases that included offsets for anticipated price increases.

and result in higher settlements that add to the problem. If the inflation does not materialize, the escalated sectors are under pressure to recoup their relative loss in future negotiations by demanding increases in excess of those provided by the formula.

To sum up: Considered in isolation, cost-of-living adjustments do not initiate inflation but intensify inflation generated by other factors. Among the "other factors" that might generate inflation are collectively bargained wage increases that originate either as "productivity" increases as part of a wage formula or from outside the escalated sector. If the system of wage determination of an economy is seen as an integrated whole, then wage formulas can contribute to a cumulative inflationary process, at least as long as they cover only a part of the economy.

This raises the sticky question of the extent to which wage settlements have initiated inflationary movements. The role of wage increases in generating inflation has been endlessly debated and usually considerably exaggerated.[15] Yet, in the writer's opinion, it is inconceivable that, in the American economy since 1945 and particularly since 1953, wage increases have not at some time and to some extent been responsible for increases in prices. The situation appears likely to recur in the future.[16] To this extent wage formulas in an economy marked by "dynamic unionism" contribute to a self-perpetuating inflation.

Summary and Conclusions

The issues raised in this chapter and the previous one can be grouped under five categories:

[15] For a comprehensive review see William G. Bowen, *The Wage-Price Issue* (Princeton University Press, 1960).

[16] Comment is in order on two arguments in rebuttal. (1) It is argued that collectively bargained wage behavior is only one factor, and not the most important one, in explaining price behavior of the 1950's. This is true, but it does not invalidate the argument in the text. (2) To the extent that wage increases have led to price increases, it is claimed that this is only because other interest groups have been permitted to exercise their economic power to prevent a transfer of income from themselves to organized wage earners. This assumes general agreement that a shift in income distribution in favor of organized wage earners is desirable on grounds of equity or the functioning of the economy. In view of the many competing claimants for increased incomes (some of them with claims vigorously supported by organized labor), this is not a self-evident conclusion.

1. Is raising wages with stable prices the appropriate method of distributing the gains in productivity that permit higher living standards?

2. What measure of productivity change should be used, what is the associated feasible rate of wage increase, and what has been the record of the past as revealed by this measure?

3. In the absence of centralized control, will the patterns of differential wage changes that are required to permit the satisfactory functioning of the economy be attainable within the framework of the productivity wage policy?

4. If a workable system of wage formulas could be devised, could it operate in the American industrial relations system with its aggressive, competitive unions?

5. Does the wage formula produce built-in inflation?

The most serious problems appear to be those related to the last three questions. With regard to the first, if the goal of price stability with rising incomes were actually to be achieved, the American economy would probably function as well under this policy as under any alternative system of wage-price relationships. The problem of measuring productivity change, pointed up by the second question, has not been solved to anyone's complete satisfaction, but improved measures are being developed, and the various alternatives seem to have established a range of variation within which there is fairly general agreement. The rate of increase in wage rates plus supplementary wage costs has probably consistently exceeded the calculated feasible rate somewhat throughout most of this century, but this behavior cannot be charged to the formula wage policy. On the contrary, more than any other single factor, the development of the wage formula touched off the most fruitful discussion of the whole wage-price problem that has ever taken place.

More serious difficulties are faced in establishing a differential rate of wage increase among occupations and industries that would meet the need for internal flexibility in the wage structure while remaining consistent with the restraints of the formula approach to wage policy in the aggregate. As far as the wage structure is concerned, the two extreme approaches that are implicit in the logic of the wage formula are both unsatisfactory. The formula approach could be interpreted as implying either uniform changes in wage rates or changes in wages by occupational class or industrial group that are exactly proportional to changes in the productivity of each class or group. Uniform changes are unworkable because they would freeze existing relationships regardless of the requirements of economic change. Because of the wide variations in rates of change in different occupations and industries and their independence of changes in the skill and effort of the workers involved, proportional changes would eventually introduce intolerable distortions in the wage structure. Between these extremes the wage formula provides no guide to wage policy on an economy-wide basis.

In itself this lack would not be critical. The difficulty is that the simplified public version of the relationship between wages and productivity encourages everyone concerned to consider the average wage-productivity relationship for the economy as a whole as the minimum standard of an equitable wage policy. Unless all wage increases are equal to the average, some must be below. If all the available wage slack is appropriated for adjustments related to productivity, then adjustments required to meet special situations of all kinds inevitably raise the average wage increase above feasible rates.[17]

Similarly, if the wage slack provided by increasing productivity is taken up by wage increases conceded by management and programmed for several years in advance, union leaders will be under strong pressure to add something to the "package" that will increase its cost beyond that permitted by the feasible rate. If this happens, the formulas will tend to produce some self-perpetuating inflation.

In the light of these criticisms, how should the formula approach to wage policy be evaluated?

Considered in the abstract as a wage policy to be applied to the whole economy, the wage formula does not offer a satisfactory solution to the problem of wage determination as this problem is usually defined. As noted earlier, most of the discussions of wage policy assume a stable price level and a continuation of the existing distribution of income by economic function. Even relaxing the assumption of stable shares and accepting as desirable the slow rate of accretion to the share of employee compensation that seems to have been characteristic of

[17] Between 1948 and 1957, in addition to wage increases included in the wage formula, GM gave certain skilled worker classifications additional increases in successive contracts. Furthermore, "special adjustments" were reported in the wage rates of "more than 116,000" other employees as part of the day-to-day administration of the wage and salary system. This is equivalent to adjusting the rates of 3 to 4 per cent of all production workers each year. General Motors, *Ten Years of Industrial Peace* (undated), p. 23.

recent years, would not change this conclusion. The systems of automatic wage adjustment have called for annual increases in real wage rates of from 2.5 to 3.5 per cent, excluding fringes, and this rate almost certainly exceeds the feasible rate that would be justified even if a gradual rise in the proportion of national income going to wage earners is projected into the future. As long as private investment is seen as the major source of economic growth, however, there is some upper limit to the share of employee compensation compatible with satisfactory levels of growth and employment. If public enterprise and public investment were to be substituted for private enterprise, the problem would change its form but not its substance. A completely socialized economy might convert all income into some type of employee compensation and solve the investment problem through direct taxation. This approach of course is already used to some extent in a "mixed" public and private enterprise economy. The feasible rate of growth in the real income of consumers would then become a problem of dividing income between public investment and private consumption (including consumption of goods and services provided through government), rather than one of dividing it three ways among public investment, private investment, and consumption, as is characteristic of a private enterprise economy.

The basic problem is that, whatever its form, any economy is limited in the increment to real personal income that is available for distribution in any time interval. If all of this increment is distributed according to a set of criteria that is incomplete because some wage-determining factors are not included, the formula will break down. If after the formula is established by the policy makers, independent decision-making units have the power to negotiate additional sector adjustments, the formula will break down. An economy with "free enterprise" and "free collective bargaining" will find unworkable in practice any national wage-adjustment system that changes money wages according to a formula including only changes in consumer prices and the average rate of productivity increase.

It should be pointed out that this is a negative evaluation of the wage formula as a full-blown national wage policy. Insofar as the principles of the formula have been portrayed as appropriate to this purpose, and in some instances this has been done, this judgment is important.

Were the analysis to stop at this point, however, the conclusion could not be extended to apply to the system as it has actually worked in the United States for the past dozen years. The fact is that the wage formula approach in practice has been limited to only a fraction of the economy, has not been applied uniformly, and has not been used continuously in some of the industries identified with it.

Any assessment of the assets and liabilities of wage formulas would be seriously incomplete unless it considered two possibilities:

1. The areas in which wage formulas have been in effect may be sectors of the economy in which above-average increases in wage rates would be accepted if a national wage policy were actually in existence. The preceding discussion stressed the inevitability of below-average wage increases in a system of differential changes in wages and emphasized the difficulty in bringing about their acceptance. It is also important to point out the inevitability of above-average wage increases in the same circumstances. A reasonable hypothesis might be that, in a system in which no formal over-all wage policy is promulgated, the sectors of the economy where below-average increases are likely to occur would be reluctant to accept this fact formally and announce it publicly in a long-term wage agreement. More buoyant sectors, on the other hand, might be expected to react differently and be more prone to use long-term contracts.

2. Even if the wage formulas as actually used should be found liable to the same criticisms as the formula as a general policy, it would be a mistake to condemn the system without considering the alternatives. Too often it is implied that, in its absence, wages would have been set by an enlightened management according to supply and demand conditions, social justice, and the public interest. During its lifetime the realistic alternative to the formulas was annual wage bargaining by powerful unions usually in periods of general prosperity.

These considerations suggest turning from the evaluation of the wage formula as a possible general wage policy to a review of its record in the context of actual events, centering on the two issues outlined above.

5

Wage Policy in Practice

THE TWO PREVIOUS chapters have considered the more important criticisms of the formula approach, most of which are aimed at its possible application as a general wage policy. It was concluded that, even if money wages, consumer prices, and productivity followed a consistent pattern in the past over the long run, any attempt to translate this experience into an *ex-ante* wage policy would face formidable obstacles. This chapter considers the way in which the various formula-type contracts have actually been applied in specific situations.

In the first sections, the history of thirteen years of experience with the wage formula is reviewed in the context of developments in industrial relations generally. This is followed by a closer inspection of the way in which the system has been implemented in those sectors of industry where the approach has been concentrated, and an attempt is made to evaluate the consequences of the interaction between these sectors and that part of the economy where other forms of wage setting have been used. Finally, the impact of the formulas is assessed in relation to the objectives sought and possible alternative ways of achieving those objectives.

The Evolution of the Formula Approach

Since 1948 the form of collective bargaining contracts in the United States has undergone some very significant changes. These changes can be summarized briefly in terms of three closely related trends. (1) By 1959 the typical collective bargaining contract had become a multi-year contract. (2) The typical multi-year contract came to call for scheduled wage adjustments in the second and later years of its term instead of providing for wage reopenings. (3) A substantial majority of the multi-year contracts with scheduled wage increases in effect at this time also include cost-of-living adjustments and qualify as formula-type contracts. After 1955 the practice of negotiating multi-year contracts with automatic wage adjustments became so prevalent and so pervasive in its effects on wage and salary adjustments in general that the years since that date could be called "the age of escalation."[1] The stages by which this situation developed are reviewed in this section.

By 1960 wage adjustment systems that compensated the worker for changes in prices and provided an annual increase in real wages had been in operation for a dozen years. Of the major contracts, however, only the pioneering GM-UAW contract of 1948 had been in effect continuously throughout the period. Until the invasion of South Korea in June 1950, the GM-UAW wage formula contract was almost unique. At the end of May 1950 the original contract was replaced by a path-breaking five-year agreement of the same general form. The company was sufficiently convinced of the usefulness of the wage-formula approach after two years of trial that it conceded a substantial nonmonetary gain to the union to secure the five-year contract. Although General Motors President Charles E. Wilson previously had expressed strong opposition in principle to compulsory union membership, the 1950 contract provided for a modified union shop. This concession was an implicit recognition of the view that American unionism may have difficulty surviving in a passive collective bargaining role. It was granted in recognition of the potential danger to the union position of five years without the drama of a wage negotiation.[2]

At the time of the Korean invasion, the GM-UAW contract ac-

---

[1] In January 1958, for example, 266 major contracts on file with the BLS were in effect. Of these, only 11 were one-year contracts and only 79 (30 per cent) did not provide for a future scheduled wage increase. "Major Agreement Expirations and Reopenings in 1958," *Monthly Labor Review* (January 1958).

[2] "You could not have a long-term agreement unless you had a flexible wage policy and have union security in our judgment." Comment by Louis G. Seaton, then Director of Labor Relations, *Proceedings*, Eighth Conference for College and University Educators (General Motors Corporation, 1954), p. 86.

The principal "modification" of the orthodox union shop was the exemption of employees who were nonmembers at the time the agreement went into effect from the necessity of joining the union. When the agreement became effective, 79 per cent of the employees in the bargaining unit were union members; by June 1954 this figure had risen to 86 per cent. The same, p. 76.

counted for about 70 per cent of the half million workers under either cost-of-living adjustments or combined escalator and scheduled increases. After the outbreak of hostilities the situation changed dramatically. Spurred by the rise in consumer prices and the probability of the imposition of wage controls, cost-of-living adjustments were inserted into a large number of contracts. By September 1950 the BLS estimated that 800,000 workers were covered by cost-of-living adjustment machinery.[3] By September 1951 this figure had risen to 3 million, and in September 1952 a high of 3.5 million was reached.

The growth in cost-of-living adjustments was not matched by a corresponding upsurge in the practice of adding "annual improvement factors" to the system in line with the GM-UAW pattern. The rest of the auto industry adopted the formula in 1950, but at the peak "more than half" of the 3.5 million workers with automatic price adjustments of some type written into their contracts were on cost-of-living escalators only and were not scheduled to receive periodic improvement-factor increases.

As hostilities came to an end in Korea in 1953 and the pace of the economy slackened later in the same year, the cost-of-living clauses began to disappear from collective bargaining agreements. By January 1955 the 3.5 million employees covered in 1953 had dropped to 1.7 million. As a rough guess, this group was composed of 1.0 to 1.2 million workers under some combination of cost-of-living and annual improvement factor adjustments, with the remainder on wage-price escalators only. During this period the great majority of the employees working under wage-formula type contracts were to be found in the automobile industry and throughout the jurisdiction of the United Auto Workers. A scanning of the BLS reports of expirations, reopenings, and wage adjustments in major collective bargaining contracts (covering more than 5,000 workers) for the years 1952, 1953, and 1954 turned up some 22 formula-type contracts covering approximately 800,000 workers with the UAW as one of the parties. Other unions were involved in 18 contracts covering about 200,000 workers.[4] Although the data are rough,

[3] The data following are from articles in the *Monthly Labor Review* by H. M. Douty, "The Growth, Status and Implications of Wage Escalation" (February 1953), pp. 126-29, and L. M. David and D. L. Helm, "Wage Escalation—Recent Developments" (March 1955), pp. 315-18.

[4] Of the 800,000 workers under UAW contracts, about 570,000 were employed by the automobile manufacturers. All of these figures are only approximations since the BLS listings used in their compilation ignore contracts covering fewer than

the general picture seems clear. Over a million workers were under formula-type contracts, about 80 per cent of them in UAW bargaining units. Most of the latter were in auto manufacturing, but almost 250,000 workers were in numerous small UAW units outside auto assembly proper. The role of the UAW is pointed up by the fact that the non-UAW contracts included some 32,000 General Motors employees represented by the International Union of Electrical Workers and included substantial numbers of contracts in farm equipment and aircraft that were directly influenced by United Automobile Workers settlements in these industries.

To sum up the first seven years of experience, General Motors pioneered the wage formula; it was accepted by the UAW as a long-term policy; the other automobile manufacturers became not overly enthusiastic converts after the invasion of Korea; and the United Automobile Workers spread variations of the approach throughout most (about 80 per cent) of its jurisdiction during the post-Korean years. Probably at no time during the period were as many as one-third of the workers under formula contracts drawn from outside the auto industry-UAW orbit.

The boom in cost-of-living adjustments unrelated to annual productivity increases that marked the Korean period fitted the classic pattern in that it represented the kind of opportunistic acceptance of this technique that has characterized other periods of substantial price inflation. Escalators were not accompanied by automatic annual increases in the typical contract and were abandoned with alacrity as prices leveled off. The existence of the GM-UAW contract at the beginning of hostilities undoubtedly hastened the adoption of cost-of-living escalators in other industries and also increased the pressures on the Wage Stabilization Board to authorize this form of wage adjustment. Experience in the United States and other countries, however, suggests that, under the circumstances at the time, cost-of-living clauses probably would have come into wide use in any event. Until 1955 the wage-for-

---

5,000 workers, do not include all those over 5,000, and provide estimates of the number of workers covered that do not apply to the same point in time. The general picture they present is probably fairly accurate, however.

Data from *Contract Expirations and Wage Adjustments in Major Agreements* (U. S. Bureau of Labor Statistics, August 29, 1952 [mimeo]; BLS Report No. 17, 1953; BLS Report No. 75, 1954).

mula contracts had had little influence on the form of wage settlements outside the UAW orbit although they undoubtedly influenced the size of some settlements.

The New 'New Era'

As noted earlier, since World War II there has been a trend away from one-year collective bargaining contracts toward multi-year agreements. Although there is no completely reliable statistical series showing the number of multi-year contracts as a proportion of all contracts in force at a given date, estimates on a fairly comparable basis by the Bureau of National Affairs indicate that in 1948 about 25 per cent of all contracts were for terms of two or more years. This figure rose to 55 per cent in 1950, 69 per cent in 1952, and 81 per cent in 1957. The U. S. Bureau of Labor Statistics found that approximately 85 per cent of the 283 major agreements in effect in 1959 specifying a fixed term were negotiated for periods of two years or longer.[5]

Until the 1953-54 recession these contracts typically provided for the reopening of the wage issue each year and did not include scheduled annual wage increases. As the economy pulled out of the recession in late 1954, a significant change in wage policy took place. Provisions for automatic future wage increases began to replace wage-reopening clauses on a large scale. The BLS survey of major agreements involving more than 5,000 workers in 1953 reported that 34 of 177 contracts called for scheduled wage increases at some future date. A survey in 1954 showed a similar picture, with 58 of 284 contracts providing for automatic increases after October 1954. A BLS survey of settlements occurring in 1955, however, described the spread of agreements on automatic increases to take place in subsequent years as "an outstanding bargaining development of that year."[6]

[5] See Jack Stieber, "Evaluation of Long-Term Contracts," in Harold Davey *et al.* (eds.), *New Dimensions in Collective Bargaining* (Harper, 1959) for a discussion of the trend prior to 1958. The 1959 figure is from the *Monthly Labor Review* (December 1958), p. 1349.

[6] BLS Reports No. 17 (June 1953) and No. 75 (October 1954); and L. M. David and D. L. Helm, "Labor-Management Contract Settlements, 1955," *Monthly Labor Review* (May 1956).

This trend gained momentum rapidly in the following years. By January 1958, 187 of the 266 major agreements in effect, covering some 4.4 million workers, provided for automatic increase in future years.[7] From a figure of less than 20 per cent in 1953 and 1954, major agreements scheduling future increases had more than tripled in four years to about 70 per cent of the total. Although the exact extent of what we have called formula-type agreements in the sense of combined cost-of-living and automatic increases is unknown, it appears that about 3.2 million workers were covered by contracts of this type.[8]

For our purposes the most significant fact about this important growth in automatic wage adjustment systems is that it was only partially in response to an inflationary movement that was already under way. To a great extent, the growing popularity of cost-of-living escalators and automatic annual increases, both separately and in combination, was the result of a deliberate decision to experiment with long-term contracts and wage formulas. It was not a defensive and pragmatic adjustment to a rapidly rising price level that these techniques had provided in the past.

Throughout the years 1953 through 1955 the Consumer Price Index had been virtually unchanged. In 1955, the year in which the spread of automatic wage increases was described as "an outstanding development," the CPI in December was almost exactly equal to the average for the year as a whole. The beginning of the much-discussed inflationary "creep" can be dated in retrospect from an 0.5 point rise in the CPI in May 1956. Before this rise occurred, the Central States Teamster

[7] "Major Agreement Expirations and Reopenings in 1958," *Monthly Labor Review* (January 1958). The data for 1959 show a similar picture. See Cordelia T. Ward, "Contract Developments Scheduled in 1959," *Monthly Labor Review* (December 1958).

[8] See "Major Agreement Expirations and Reopenings in 1958," *Monthly Labor Review* (January 1958) and "Deferred Increases and Escalator Clauses," *Monthly Labor Review* (December 1958).

It is very difficult to arrive at a completely unambiguous figure for the number of workers covered by both types of clauses. The major source of confusion is illustrated by the way the 3.2 million estimate was derived. The December 1958 *Review* article cited above notes that about 1.6 million workers were employed under agreements that provided for both types of adjustments in 1959. But this excludes over 1 million railroad workers and about 0.5 million steelworkers because their escalator contracts were expiring in 1959 and hence did not call for an automatic increase. They were included nevertheless since our aim is to estimate the prevalence of this type of contract in general, not to estimate the number getting increases in any specific time period.

long-term agreements included a type of wage formula for about 170,000 workers in early 1955, the automobile-UAW group of wage-formula agreements expired and were renewed in June 1955, and the electrical equipment industry adopted formula-type contracts beginning with General Electric in August 1955. Other major contracts providing for some form of automatic adjustments, although not both parts of the formula, were to be found in the construction industry, in some printing agreements, and in some textile agreements.

In 1956 the steel industry proposed a wage settlement similar to the wage formula in July. This can hardly be regarded as a reaction to price inflation since it occurred at a time when the latest available Consumer Price Index change was the initial 0.5 point rise in May.[9] The importance of price inflation in the negotiation of the meat-packing formula agreements in the early fall of 1956 is difficult to assess. By November 1956, when the railroads introduced cost-of-living escalation and annual increases in three-year contracts, the inflationary trend had been in evidence for five months, and there is little doubt that these agreements and later ones were in part the result of the observed and anticipated behavior of prices.

The point of this argument is that the year 1955 marks the beginning of an important experiment in American industrial relations. For the first time a major cross section of American industry tentatively adopted a contract system—based on the postulate underlying the formula wage policy—that long-term contracts protecting the money wage from inflation and scheduling substantial automatic wage increases for years in advance might be the basis of a workable long-range wage policy. The formula approach at this time was not primarily a defensive reaction to price inflation, actual or anticipated.

There were a number of reasons for the rapid spread of the practice of scheduling automatic wage increases of all types in the multi-year contracts from about one-fifth of major agreements in 1953-54 to over two-thirds in 1958. The most important of these seem to be (1) the growing confidence that major depressions might be avoided in the future; (2) the acceptance of the continued existence of aggressive labor unions in the major organized areas of the economy; and (3) the desire

[9] It could be argued that the CPI had been stable but that for some months the prices of most nonagricultural goods had been trending upward, and that this may have led to inflationary expectations.

to experiment with long-term contracts and automatic wage setting. Although the first two are not directly related to the object of this study, a few comments on them are in order since the three factors are interrelated to a very significant degree.

Confidence in the Stability of the Economy

Without producing rigorous documentation, it appears that at some point in the postwar period, employers as a whole became convinced that the deflationary collapses that had followed major wars in the past would not be repeated. The relative mildness of the 1949 recession probably convinced some. By 1952 Clark Kerr was commenting on the faith that employers had developed in government's ability to protect them from the consequences of deflation and pointing out that "their faith in government is a faith that moves wage levels."[10] The brief duration of the 1953-54 recession undoubtedly reinforced the convinced in their beliefs and enlisted new converts. By 1955 the American economy had experienced ten years of fairly high-level postwar prosperity and had weathered two minor recessions. The basis for concluding that a new economic era based on government's commitment to stability and on industry's rationalized long-range planning was at hand. The investment boom of 1955-56, the behavior of the stock market, and the new wage policy are all testimony to the validity of the conclusion that a "new era" philosophy was in vogue.

The Impact of Aggressive Unionism

Probably a majority of the employers in the major organized sectors of the American economy had resigned themselves to dealing with entrenched unions prior to 1955. Many of them, however, cherished the hope that a shift in the balance of power in collective bargaining might be imminent, as a result either of changed governmental policy, or of economic depression, or both. By 1955 it was evident that the Taft-Hartley Act of 1947 had not significantly weakened established

[10] Clark Kerr, "Governmental Wage Restraints: Their Limits and Uses in a Mobilized Economy," *American Economic Review* (May 1952), p. 370.

unions and that the contemporary Republican administration was not likely to alter substantially the relative positions of the parties to collective bargaining. The failure of a major postwar depression to materialize, coupled with the continued, though moderated, upward pressures on wages during the two recessions, led to a reassessment of the likelihood that major changes in bargaining strength would take place in the near future. If the annual wage reopenings that the then-existing collective bargaining contracts called for were to result in a monotonous succession of yearly wage increases, it made sense to consider scheduling raises in advance to avoid repeated negotiations and potential strikes.

Influence of Wage-Formula Contracts

Once the probability of relatively continuous high levels of economic activity and the persistence of rising wage trends is conceded, the attractiveness of the pattern of long-term wage agreements of the wage-formula type is obvious. C. E. Wilson's argument that such contracts were simply methods of doing on purpose what probably would otherwise be done by accident, acquired considerable plausibility. In addition, in a later section it will be argued that the deductive nature of this type of speculation was reinforced by the good record compiled by users of the formula approach during a period that included two recessions and a major "police action."

As a result of the combined effect of these considerations, by 1958-59 almost 5 million workers were covered by some type of annual automatic wage increase plan, and about 70 per cent of these employees were working under one or the other version of the formula.

This is not to say that the companies and unions negotiating these agreements subscribed to the fairly elaborate rationale of the wage formula outlined in Chapter 2. Few of them bothered to rationalize their new wage policy, at least publicly. In particular, there were few references to relating annual increases to changes in productivity for the economy as a whole. If pressed, they might have put forth some simple version of the ideas behind the wage formula, but in general the approach seems to have been one of experimentation and pattern following. Although many variations developed, the essentials of the pattern being followed were those of the original GM-UAW wage formula agreement, i.e., relatively frequent wage adjustment to compensate for price changes, coupled with scheduled annual increases.

The Formulas in Action

In the previous sections the "age of escalation" was described as beginning in 1955. Prior to that year the formula wage policy was shown to be virtually a monopoly of the automobile industry and the United Automobile Workers, particularly the latter. In that year a rapid growth occurred, with contracts combining cost-of-living and automatic annual adjustments more than tripling in coverage as they spread into other major areas of the economy. The outlines of this pattern of development were obscured by the widespread adoption of cost-of-living adjustments without other automatic wage changes during the Korean episode. These arrangements disappeared rapidly with the ending of hostilities, however, leaving behind the hard core of the formula approach, the automobile industry and the UAW.

In the upsurge of formula-type contracts after 1955, the reader will have observed that the major share of the total employee coverage could be found in a handful of industries. In round numbers and in the order of their adoption of the system, the auto (600,000), trucking (200,000), electrical equipment (150,000), steel (500,000), and railroad (1,000,000) industries accounted for something close to 70 to 75 per cent of all the covered workers.

This suggests that a useful way to begin an assessment of the workings of this approach would be to review the record of its operation in some of these industries.

The Automobile Industry[11]

During the period 1948-50, Chrysler and Ford engaged in annual wage bargaining while General Motors was operating under the first of

---

[11] Unless otherwise stated, data in this section are from "Major Settlements in the Automobile Industry, 1949-1950," *Monthly Labor Review* (August 1950), pp. 222-24; and BLS, Wage Chronologies No. 5, Supplement 1; No. 9, Supplements 1 and 2; and No. 14, Supplements 1 and 2.

the wage-formula contracts. The pattern of developments in the two systems was quite different, but of course this cannot be attributed solely to this single factor. Nevertheless, this experience is worth reviewing.

General Motors and the United Automobile Workers signed the first formula contract in May 1948, including in it an initial wage adjustment of 11 cents an hour. By May 1950, the terminal date of the agreement, the cost-of-living adjustments had produced a net drop of 2 cents in base rates. At the midpoint of the contract period in June 1949, however, an improvement factor adjustment of 3 cents was added to base rates so that the net change from the combined effect of the two parts of the wage formula was a gain of 1 cent in base rates. The cost of the formula to the corporation for this period cannot be measured by the net change in rates between the two terminal dates. During part of the period wage rates were as much as 3 cents above the initial level, and, on the average, base rates were 2.1 cents higher for the two years considered as a whole than they were after the original 11 cent increase in May 1948.[12] Put differently, the direct effect on wage cost of the wage settlement in the 1948 contract (including the 11-cent general increase) was equivalent to a 13-cent wage increase granted at the beginning of the period.

Turning to the Ford and Chrysler settlements in 1948, it is a little startling to find that both contracts provided for a 13-cent general wage increase. The 1948 Ford agreement had a one-year term, while the Chrysler contract was to run for two years with a reopening, but in neither case were general wage increases granted in 1949.

Important nonwage issues were settled during 1949-50. The Ford renegotiation and the 1949 Chrysler reopening centered around the ques-

---

[12] This figure was calculated by averaging the adjustment in effect in each quarter, assuming that the May 1949 cost-of-living adjustment went into effect simultaneously with the improvement factor of that year. (Actually the latter preceded the former by one week.)

Contract quarter	Cumulated formula adjustment	Contract quarter	Cumulated formula adjustment
1	0	5	3
2	3	6	3
3	3	7	3
4	1	8	1
			$17 \div 8 = 2.1$

tion of pensions and group insurance. Ford and the UAW reached an agreement at the end of September that provided a pension and insurance package estimated to cost 10 cents an hour. After protracted negotiations and a 100-day strike, a settlement similar to the Ford agreement was reached at Chrysler in May 1950. Its cost was estimated at 10 cents by the union. (Estimates of the cost of insurance programs, particularly pensions, are highly tentative.) General Motors added a similar (though somewhat more generous) welfare benefit package in its new five-year agreement negotiated shortly after the Chrysler settlement.

Before the first two years of operation of the formula are assessed, the provisions of the new Ford and Chrysler contracts should be examined. The September 1949 Ford agreement did not provide for a general wage increase. It was a three-year contract with annual reopenings on wages. The May 1950 settlement at Chrysler also was a three-year agreement with annual reopenings, but with no wage increase in 1950. In contrast, the 1950 GM contract called for an immediate improvement-factor adjustment of 4 cents. After this raise, the wage increases since 1948 totaled 16 cents for General Motors and 13 cents each for the other two companies.

It would have been very informative to follow the pattern of wage changes generated by the two sets of wage adjusting systems over the next few years. But this was not possible because the invasion of Korea led to a complete revision of bargaining arrangements. By December 1950, both Ford and Chrysler had changed their original agreements and had adopted the General Motors pattern, with the wage formula written into new contracts to end in 1955. In the process, wage changes were manipulated so that the increases in base rates exactly equalled the change in GM rates since 1948 (24 cents by December 1950). In effect, Ford and Chrysler adopted the General Motors wage formula retroactive to 1948.

There is little in this record to suggest that the existence of the GM wage formula had any significant influence on wage developments in the auto industry prior to the invasion of South Korea. The decision of the UAW to press for pensions and insurance benefits in 1949 was not related to the existence of the GM contract. The 3-cent improvement factor increase in 1949 may have contributed to a feeling that some increase was "in the air," but the actual settlements in 1949 were so different in form and in amount as to suggest that this influence was negligible. It might be argued that over the two years the GM settlements provide a classic example of "whipsawing" in that General Motors gave a 3-cent money increase in 1949 and then was forced into the 1949 pension pattern in 1950. If the Ford reopening in September 1950 had produced a money settlement that brought the Ford workers close to the total of 7 cents given by GM in the combined 1949 and 1950 improvement factors, the case for calling this "whipsawing" would be a strong one. (The issue would have been complicated by the erosion of 2 of the 3 cents of the 1949 improvement factor by price changes.) Unfortunately, by September 1950 the outbreak of hostilities intervened to prevent the testing of this hypothesis. On balance, it would appear that the 1949-50 bargaining in autos followed a pattern, but that the pattern was apparently unrelated to the GM-UAW agreement.

Because the several auto industry settlements since 1950 have been very similar and the interim adjustments have followed the same formula, we turn to a brief analysis of the wage history of the industry as a whole. From 1948 to 1961 the cost-of-living clause has retained its basic concept unchanged. Every three months wage rates have been adjusted to offset price changes as measured by the Consumer Price Index currently in use. The improvement factor was increased from 3 to 4 cents in 1950, to 5 cents in 1953, and to 6 cents or 2.5 per cent, whichever is larger in each individual case, in 1955. (From 1948 to 1955 the factor in cents was adjusted to represent about 2 per cent of the rising average hourly earnings.)

The most appropriate readily available measure of the effect on wage costs of the productivity wage policy as it actually worked out is the behavior of gross average hourly earnings (AHE). Table 2 presents data on the annual rates of change in prices, earnings, and productivity between 1948 and 1959.

During this eleven-year period, AHE in the automobile industry increased at an annual rate of 4.8 per cent. Corrected for price changes, real AHE increased 3 per cent per year. These results can be usefully compared either with some measure of change in productivity or with changes in earnings in other industries.

There are no productivity data available for the automobile industry, but the increases in real AHE in autos roughly matched the rate of increase in real product per man-hour in the private economy, some-

TABLE 2. *Prices, Productivity, and Earnings, 1948–59*

Item	1948	1959	Annual Rate of Increase (per cent)
1. Consumer price index	102.8	124.6	1.8
2. Productivity: Real product/MH Manufacturing			
All persons	100.1	127.7 (1957)	2.7
Production workers	99.7	137.4 (1957)	3.6
Total private economy	100.2	135.4 (1958)	3.1
3. All manufacturing: AHE	$1.35	$2.22	4.6
Real AHE	—	—	2.8
4. Durable goods: AHE	$1.41	$2.38	4.9
Real AHE	—	—	3.1
5. Motor vehicles and parts: AHE	$1.61*	$2.70	4.8
Real AHE	—	—	3.0
Real AHE plus increases in fringes**	—	—	4.0
6. Blast furnaces, steel works, etc.: AHE	$1.58	$3.08	6.3
Real AHE	—	—	4.4
7. Electrical machinery: AHE	$1.39	$2.22	4.3
Real AHE	—	—	2.5
8. Meat products: AHE	$1.35	$2.36	5.2
Real AHE	—	—	3.4
9. Bldg. construction: AHE	$1.85	$3.22	5.1
Real AHE	—	—	3.3
10. Rubber tires and tubes: AHE	$1.67	$2.92	5.2
Real AHE	—	—	3.4

Sources: (1)   BLS, *Monthly Labor Review*, March 1953 and November 1960, Tables D-1.
        (2)   BLS, *Trends in Output per Man-Hour in the Private Economy, 1909–1958*, Bulletin No. 1249, pp. 5, 40.
        (3)–(10), BLS, *Monthly Labor Review*, November 1949 and November 1960, Tables C-1. Gross average hourly earnings of production workers (AHE).
        (5)   * The figure for 1948 is for "automobiles," a more inclusive classification than "motor vehicles and parts." The effect is to understate 1948 AHE and overstate slightly the rate of increase.
        (6)   ** Calculated by arbitrarily adding $.30 to 1959 AHE as an estimate of the cost of fringes *added* during 1948–59. This overstates the percentage increase since an unknown amount of fringe costs should be in the base figures for both years.
        All data are annual averages. Indexes on base 1947–49. Rates of change computed by compound interest formula.

what exceeded the rate for real product per man-hour of "all persons" employed in manufacturing, and was substantially below the rate of increase for production workers in all manufacturing.[13]

To show the effect of including at least some of the costs of fringe benefits on total costs, an estimate of the rate of increase in AHE plus a rough estimate of the increase in fringe costs between 1948 and 1959 has been included in Table 2. On this basis, it appears that the rate of increase in total compensation (earnings plus fringes) of about 4 per cent exceeded the increase in all the productivity measures listed. Whether it also exceeded the increase in productivity for the automobile industry is an unanswerable question.[14]

Turning to comparisons with trends in earnings in other industries, we find that real AHE in autos increased slightly faster than in all manufacturing and at about the same rate as in durable goods manufacturing. Of the several other industries included in Table 2, automobile AHE increased less rapidly than the AHE of steel, meat products, building construction, and rubber tires and tubes, but more rapidly than electrical machinery.

Although any assessment of this behavior must be subjective, the following conclusions seem to be justified:

1. As far as the increase in direct wages (either rates or earnings) is concerned, the automobile industry's wage policy accomplished its objective of relating wage changes to over-all increases in productivity for the economy on the average over the long run.

2. If an estimate of the increase of the cost of fringes is added, the rate of increase in hourly compensation exceeded the feasible rate as measured by productivity gains. How serious this divergence is depends on a judgment as to the appropriate measure of productivity change. If productivity per production-worker man-hour is used, the rate of increase for compensation is about 10 per cent per year higher than the rate of increase in productivity. Use of the other productivity measures yields larger differentials.

[13] Information on real product for labor and capital combined is not available for manufacturing. For the total private economy, the annual rate was 2.1 per cent from 1948 to 1957. See Table 2.

[14] The reader is reminded that under some circumstances all fringe costs should not be added to AHE when making wage-productivity comparisons. The arbitrary 30 cent estimate added in Table 2 is quite conservative.

3. Compared with other major industries, some of which are related to the automobile industry and some not, the wage record in autos is a relatively modest one.

No one can know what would have happened in this industry under other circumstances, but the results of the formula wage policy in autos would seem to have been not very different from the results that would have followed from a continuation of annual wage bargaining. Note that this is a relative statement and does not imply anything about the absolute effects of wage bargaining on possible inflationary pressures.

This judgment coincides with those expressed to the writer by both management and union representatives in the automobile industry. Both groups feel that the magnitude of wage changes, on the average, have been affected to only a slight extent, if at all, by the wage formula. In spite of this, some of the company representatives expressed a vague dissatisfaction with formula bargaining. This seemed to be based on a feeling that the formula approach had frozen the various companies into an undesirable uniformity of policy for an indefinite period. The likelihood that, in the absence of formula bargaining, the UAW would accept settlements from individual companies that were significantly different in their cost effects would not seem to be very great.

An important exception to this generalization might be some sort of profit-sharing scheme. Reuther has proposed a version of profit-sharing, and some comments by two company representatives suggested that a new "wage formula" that tied wages to individual company performance instead of to "productivity" would be viewed with interest. Management seems to be thinking of the two formulas as alternatives, however, while Reuther sees them as complementing one another. (Since this was originally written, American Motors and the UAW negotiated a form of profit-sharing in 1961, at the same time retaining the formula.)

This analysis suggests that the price paid for the long-term agreements under the GM wage formula has been somewhat but not substantially higher than was indicated by the rationale of the system. It is pertinent to ask what the parties to the system, particularly management, have received in return.

The most dramatic single fact about industrial relations in the automobile industry would seem to be this: No company-wide strike occurred among the Big Three producers between 1950 and 1961. General Motors' last company-wide strike was the 1945-46 stoppage; Ford suffered something close to a company-wide strike in May 1949 over production standards during the term of an existing contract; the last major strike at Chrysler occurred in the Spring of 1950 over the funding of pension liability. No one would claim that this record is due entirely to the existence of the wage formula,[15] but the long-term contracts have certainly played a major role. It is not necessary to view industrial conflict as a probability process to attach considerable weight to the fact that, between 1950 and 1961, there were only three full-fledged negotiations and to conclude that this reduced the "exposure" of the industry to large-scale strikes very substantially. Anyone who had predicted at the conclusion of the GM strike in the Spring of 1946 that there would not be another major strike over wages in the automobile industry for at least sixteen years certainly would have been regarded as a visionary.

From the union's point of view, the wage formula assured it of a quick, painless adjustment to changing prices, guaranteed an annual wage increase, and provided an over-all rate of increase in real wages that would double real wages in about eighteen years.

These results suggest that, assuming satisfactory performance of the economy as a whole and the automobile industry in particular, the industry is likely to be reluctant to heed exhortations to abandon the formula and the long-term contract and to bargain at frequent intervals.[16] Greater flexibility in bargaining policy might well be desirable in the general case, but the dynamics of institutional relationships will continue to tempt confident managers with a proven record of competence to exchange potential flexibility for partial predictability. The automobile industry's experience indicates that it is possible to chance such a policy with considerable success.

The Steel Industry

During the first two postwar years steel industry wage bargaining was an integral part of the general surge of the first two "rounds" of wage

[15] See A. M. Ross and P. Hartman, *The Changing Nature of Industrial Conflict* (Wiley, 1960) for an argument that overt conflict in general is withering away. By 1961 it was becoming harder to identify a "company-wide" strike. Some observers might class GM's difficulties in 1958 as such, but the writer of this study would not agree. The 1961 strike would qualify as a company-wide strike, but wages were not a primary issue.

[16] See, for example, Benson Soffer, "The Decline of Collective Bargaining on General Wage Increases," *California Management Review* (September 1959), p. 54,

increases.[17] The contract which concluded the 1947 steel negotiations was rather unusual in that it provided for a reopening in 1948 but did not permit the union to strike in the event an impasse in bargaining was reached. Before the reopening in April 1948, U. S. Steel announced a no-increase wage policy and appeared to be prepared to stick to this decision. At the same time negotiations in the automobile industry were deadlocked. The latter stalemate was broken in May 1948 with the negotiation of the first of the GM-UAW formula agreements. Following the automobile settlements, steel fell reluctantly in line, meeting the 13-cent pattern of Ford and Chrysler. From this time until 1956, except for an off-schedule settlement at the time of Korea, basic steel wage bargaining produced a series of two-year contracts with annual reopenings on wages. In August 1956 steel began operating under a three-year contract with a cost-of-living escalator and annual increases. The mid-1948 to mid-1956 period, during which the steel industry negotiated wages annually, provides an excellent case study of the functioning of this system.

Between 1948 and 1956, the steel industry increased its minimum base rate a total of 74 cents while gross average hourly earnings rose 96 cents from about $1.52 in June 1948 (the month before the 1948 wage increase) to $2.48 in June 1956.[18]

and Jules Backman, "Wage Escalation and Wage Inflation," *Industrial and Labor Relations Review* (April 1960), p. 410.

[17] Wage information in this section is from U. S. Bureau of Labor Statistics, *Wage Chronology No. 3* and supplements and the *Monthly Labor Review*. Other material from the Bureau of National Affairs, *Collective Bargaining Negotiations and Contracts*, 18:47-48g.

[18] A comment on the meaning of these figures is necessary. Since 1947, jobs in steel have been grouped into 32 labor grades or classes for pay purposes. The basic wage change reported in contemporary accounts of settlements usually is the increase to be applied to the lowest paid labor grade (grade one or in recent years one and two combined). General wage increases since (and including) 1947, except those of 1953 and 1954, have not only raised each labor grade by the stated amount, but have added to this basic increase an increment designed to increase the differential between grades. For example, the 1958 increase of 7 cents that was scheduled in the 1956 contract was coupled with an increment of 0.2 cents to the differential between each grade so that the top labor grade actually received an increase of 13 cents (7 + [30 × .2] = 13).

A majority of steelworkers are paid on an incentive basis which provides bonus overtime rates related to production levels. (The *Monthly Labor Review* for May 1960 [p. 461] reports 60 per cent.) This typically results in hourly earnings that are a multiple of base rates for that labor grade. For these jobs an increase in the

In terms of an annual rate of change, this meant an impressive gain of 6.4 per cent per year in hourly earnings over this period. By contrast, earnings in the automobile industry rose at a considerably slower rate, 5.1 per cent annually (See Table 3.) As a result of these differential rates of increase in earnings, the average hourly earnings of steelworkers rose from 3 cents below auto workers earnings in 1948 to

TABLE 3. *Increases in Earnings and Productivity in Basic Steel and Motor Vehicles, 1948–59*

Item	Average Annual Rates of Change (Per Cent)	
	mid-1948* to mid-1956	mid-1956 to mid-1959
Blast furnaces, etc.—AHE	6.4	7.8
Real AHE	4.7	5.4
Motor vehicles—AHE	5.1	5.2
Real AHE	3.5	2.7
Output/Man-hour, Basic steel	1948–59**	
All employees	2.8	
Wage employees	3.4	

* "mid" refers to May in the case of automobiles and June for steel.
** Computed by using figures for the calendar year 1948 and the fiscal year ending June 1959.
Sources: Wage data from *Monthly Labor Review*, Tables C-1. Output per man-hour data from Otto Eckstein and Gary Fromm, *Steel and the Postwar Inflation*, Study Paper No. 2, Study of Employment, Growth, and Price Levels, Joint Economic Committee (Nov. 6, 1959), p. 21.
Note: Earnings data differ from those given in Table 2 because of different time periods covered. Only substantial differences in rates of change within each table should be considered significant because of the effects of varying terminal dates.

job wage rate has a magnified effect on actual earnings. An estimate of the cost effect from this source is included in the rate changes after 1956 noted in the text.

To illustrate the effect of these two factors, in 1958 the basic rate change was 7 cents, the cost of the increment to job grades was estimated to add 1.29 cents, and the incentive effect to add 0.83 cents to hourly wage costs. (Estimates were obtained from company data by the United Steelworkers.) Estimates of rate changes in the text include all three elements for a total of 9.1 cents in 1958 while earnings figures include all three plus the effects of some fringes, such as premium pay for overtime, Sundays, and holidays.

The fact that the increment effect and the incentive effect both operate to increase the basic rate change agreed on is important in interpreting steel wage changes under the formula-type contract.

An additional complication in interpreting earnings figures like those in Table 3 is that the steel industry's installation of a comprehensive job evaluation plan over several years tended to raise earnings. (See Jack Stieber, *The Steel Industry Wage Structure* [Harvard University Press, 1959].)

18 cents above in 1956.[19] Not only had steel earnings increased substantially more than auto earnings, but real earnings in steel had increased substantially more than productivity in steel, even without taking into account any fringe benefit costs.

While this impressive record of wage gains was being accumulated, the industry had undergone an industry-wide strike of 42 days in 1949, a short strike in April 1952, a 55-day strike in June-July 1952, and a brief stoppage in 1955. In contrast, no major automobile company had undergone a strike over wages since adopting the wage-formula approach.

Under the circumstances, it is not surprising that the steel industry decided in 1956 to experiment with a long-term contract of the wage-formula type. Significantly a 34-day strike was required before the 1956 negotiations could produce the steel industry's version of the wage formula. The resulting contract provided for a cost-of-living adjustment clause which became operative at six-month intervals and average direct wage increases of 10.5, 9.1, and 9.1 cents to go into effect in July 1956, 1957, and 1958.

Since average hourly earnings in basic steel were $2.48 at the time the contract was signed, the annual increases called for in this contract were just under 4 per cent of the 1956 earnings. This meant that they were substantially above the 2.5-per cent annual improvement factor of the automobile wage formula.

It is interesting that the increases in the three settlements prior to 1956 (1955, 1954, and 1953), all of which were reached in annual bargaining, averaged approximately 9.5 cents. In effect, the 1956 contract provided the union in each of the next three years with the same average wage increase that had been negotiated in annual bargaining during the three previous years and added a cost-of-living clause to the package. (Other components of the settlement, such as the supplementary unemployment benefits plan, are being ignored.)

With the advantage of hindsight, this can be seen as an unfortunate decision from the companies' point of view. In addition to the almost 4 per cent annual increase scheduled in each year of the contract, the

[19] The figures are $1.52 and $1.55 for steel and auto workers respectively in 1948 and $2.48 and $2.30 in 1956. The 21-cent relative gain by the steelworkers was due partly to larger basic rate increases (about 12 cents from this source) and the rest from the combined effect of other wage administration policies, including the incentive pay system and job increments.

cost-of-living adjustment had generated a total wage increase of 17 cents by January 1959. As a result, the steel industry's trial of the formula approach produced a three-year total direct wage increase of about 46 cents and an over-all package increase of an estimated 63 cents (including fringe costs), according to company figures. As Table 3 indicates, steel's three-year, formula-type contract resulted in a rate of increase in both real and money wages that significantly exceeded the rates characteristic of the 1948-56 period. In discussions with the writer, both union and management representatives agreed that annual wage bargaining would have produced a lower total settlement over the 1956-59 period, largely because of the effect of the 1957-58 recession.

As the 1956 contract neared its end in 1959, the steel industry and the union engaged in vigorous bargaining activity, culminating in a lengthy strike, presidential intervention, a fact-finding board, Taft-Hartley injunctions, and the rest of the paraphernalia of a crisis in industrial relations. Although nonwage issues played a critical role in the total situation, it was evident that management hoped to eliminate the cost-of-living escalator from the final settlement. The resulting thirty-month contract retained the form but little of the substance of the cost-of-living adjustment. The companies agreed to take over the cost of the employee share of insurance benefits immediately, and scheduled two future annual increases in direct wages during the life of the contract.[20] On the whole, the contract signed in January 1960 called for

---

[20] The last cost-of-living adjustment under the 1956 contract went into effect in January 1959. The new contract was signed in January 1960, by which time the price-escalator formula indicated that a 4-cent increase would have been in order. The new contract ignored this factor and provided for a cost-of-living increase in October 1960 that could not exceed 3 cents and that would be reduced to offset increases in monthly insurance costs that might have occurred in that time. In August 1961, the same procedure, subject to the same limitations, was to be followed. In effect, during the term of the contract, cost-of-living adjustments are limited to 6 cents, less offsets to counterbalance increases in insurance costs.

Other direct wage increases scheduled were an average of 8.6 cents on December 1, 1960 and an average of 7.9 cents on October 1, 1960. These estimates include the "increment" but not the "incentive" effects. The industry estimated that the total increase in direct wage costs for the 30 months would be 21.5 cents, with additional costs of 7 cents to make the insurance plans noncontributory as of January 1960. This suggests that the annual cost of the scheduled direct wage increases of the 1959 contract is not far from the cost of the 1956 contract in cents-per-hour terms and somewhat less in percentage terms. The limitation of the price adjustment probably will make an important difference, however.

Data are from the company and union "Memorandum of Agreement" and *Business Week* (Jan. 9, 1960), p. 76.

annual increases in wages that were not much different from those of the 1956 contract, but it drastically limited the possible gains from cost-of-living adjustments.

It is apparent that the experience of the steel industry with its version of the wage formula has not engendered enthusiastic support for the principle. There appear to be several reasons for dissatisfaction with this wage policy in steel.

1. To some extent, the 1956 contract suffered from some unfortunate timing. It was preceded by almost three years of price stability that had minimized the effect of cost-of-living clauses in other contracts. The new experiment, however, was launched in a prosperous year right at the beginning of a substantial rise in the Consumer Price Index, the magnitude of which was at least partly unanticipated. During the term of the agreement a sharp recession occurred, which emphasized the cost burden of the wage increases. Had the industry been bargaining annually on wages, at least one bargaining session would have taken place during a depressed period and would probably have produced a smaller settlement. Whereas the early experience of GM and the UAW came during a period of price stability, steel's introduction to the formula system coincided with a substantial price rise.

2. The characteristics of the wage structure and the wage payment system in the steel industry worked to increase substantially the apparent cost of settlements. The minimum wage rate increase for the lowest paid labor grade in the steel wage structure was itself somewhat above the annual improvement factor increase in the automobile industry, and its size may have reflected inter-union competition between the UAW and the Steelworkers. At the same time the multiplicity of job classes in steel and the desire to increase absolute differentials between classes added another cost element to the settlement. The prevalence of incentive pay systems meant that still another increase in wage costs was built into the pay system. The wage data in this section suggest that the nominal wage increase in steel settlements has been expanded by almost one-third by these two elements.

The problems of wage administration exemplified by the need to maintain differentials between occupations are present in the automobile industry as well, but the effect is less serious because of what appears to be a simpler wage structure, infrequent use of wage incentives, and less frequent realignment of wage differentials.

3. Probably the most important reason for the dissatisfaction of the industry with this approach was that the parties failed to accept the "rationale" of the wage formula proper and to tailor their settlement to its requirements. Partly because of the economic situation at the time of its introduction, the GM-UAW wage formula represents an agreement in principle on the rate of real wage increase that is accepted as "normal," at least for the duration of any given contract. The union, which repeatedly has publicly enunciated a policy of "progress with the community," accepted the economy-wide rate of increase in productivity (imprecisely defined) as at least a partial standard for wage policy. The union has challenged the size of the particular rate of increase built into the formula, but it has not attacked the principle. Thirteen years after the introduction of the formula, the improvement factor was still 2.5 per cent, a figure probably fairly close to the "feasible rate" of wage increase justified by the past behavior of the economy. At periodic renegotiations of the contract, the union and the auto industry bargain over the question of the additional increase in real wages, if any, that will be negotiated. If the productivity performance of the automobile industry should lag behind that of the economy or if the industry should be under economic pressure from other sources, the extra gains will become smaller or nonexistent.

In steel, on the other hand, the 1956 contract projected a rate of wage increase into the future that was as high as, or higher than, the rate that had prevailed in past bargaining. This rate was also higher than the productivity gain in either steel or the economy as a whole. This pattern of increase was rendered "inflation-proof" by the addition of the Consumer Price Index escalator. In effect, the industry paid the price of assuming the risk of future price increases in return for a long-term contract. As events worked out, this was a costly bargain.

Although the issue was confused by the handling of the work practices dispute, in 1959 the industry chose to expend a major part of its bargaining power to reduce the price paid for a multi-year contract by eliminating or reducing the potential cost of the escalator. This approach was adopted in preference to the other obvious policies of returning to annual wage bargaining or retaining the escalator but reducing the average (not the minimum) wage rate increase to something like the 2.5 per cent characteristic of the automobile industry wage-formula contracts. The behavior of the Consumer Price Index over the term of the contract will determine the comparative costs of the policy that was adopted and the second alternative above. In assessing these alternatives, the reader should note that as long as the steel contracts schedule wage changes in cents-per-hour terms, the effect of rising earnings levels is to reduce the annual rate of wage change in percentage terms. The 1959 contracts raise direct wage costs at a rate not much different from the 1956 contracts in cents-per-hour, but the higher AHE currently being paid means that the percentage rate of increase has been cut to about 3 per cent a year.

Two final points should be made:

1. Steel production is more basic to the economy than is automobile production. The two long-term contracts in steel have been signed after lengthy strikes in which political intervention was substantial even though the administration in power was opposed to such intervention in principle. There is considerable agreement that the effect of this intervention has been to raise settlements above the levels that might otherwise have been reached.[21] This helps to explain the wage history of the industry in the past. Since the tendency toward "politicalizing" steel bargaining is unlikely to decrease and may well increase in the future, the pressures to rationalize collective bargaining and achieve viable long-term contracts will continue to be very strong.

2. Even if the formula-type contract were to disappear from the steel industry, it appears inevitable that movements in consumer prices and changes in productivity will continue to play a major role in negotiations. If bargaining is predominantly private in nature, it is hard to believe that movements in the CPI and trends in productivity will not be major determinants of settlements. When governmental representatives participate, formally or informally, these standards are even more likely to be called upon to resolve differences. Price and wage policies in steel seem destined to take on even more of a quasi-public utility character than they have in the past. In these circumstances, the appeal

[21] Reviewing these effects, Eckstein and Fromm conclude, "There can be little doubt that the effect of Government has been to increase the rate of increase of wages." Otto Eckstein and Gary Fromm, *Steel and the Postwar Inflation*, Study Paper No. 2, Study of Employment, Growth, and Price Levels, Joint Economic Committee (Nov. 6, 1959), p. 20.

to explicit criteria for wage setting is almost irresistible, and the factors behind the formula wage policy seem likely to continue to influence settlements in one form or another.

The Electrical Machinery Industry[22]

The other major industry whose bargaining pattern will be reviewed in this chapter is the electrical machinery equipment industry. Several factors prevent the analysis of this industry from being as clear-cut as that of the steel and auto industries. The most difficult problems arise because the industry is much more heterogeneous in its product-mix, its company structure, and its union organization than is either basic steel or autos. Many of the companies in the industry compete in only some of the separate submarkets of the industry as a whole. In addition, it has been a particularly dynamic sector of the economy, changing the nature and types of products produced, the manufacturing process, and the composition of its labor force during the postwar period.

The issue is complicated further by the fact that the companies in the industry are reluctant to release average hourly earnings figures. (There are no wage chronologies from the industry included in the BLS series, for example.) Wage adjustments are usually announced in percentage rather than cents-per-hour terms. Even the cost-of-living adjustments under the wage contracts are stated in percentages.

The industry is of interest because it shows a different pattern from either the steel or auto industries. Like steel, the industry bargained more or less on an annual basis during the early years of the period under consideration and then shifted to a version of the formula. A unique element in the situation, however, is that General Motors is a major employer in the electrical equipment industry proper. The electrical equipment divisions of GM account for about 10 per cent, or some 35,000, of General Motors' production employees, a substantial figure though one that ranked GM well behind General Electric and

[22] Material in this section is from the *Monthly Labor Review* and the Bureau of National Affairs, *Collective Bargaining Negotiations and Contracts*, 18: 20-20e. Statements about company and union attitudes are derived from interviews with GE executives and an exchange of correspondence with the Director of Economics and Research of the IUE.

Westinghouse as an employer in the postwar years. The GM segment of the industry has been under basically the same wage-formula con-tracts as the automobile workers since 1948. This has had an important impact on the wage patterns of the other employers.

The relatively decentralized character of collective bargaining, the presence of strongly competitive unions since 1949, and the tie-in with the automobile industry make this industry a logical candidate for study.

Although the wage record is not completely unambiguous, there ap-pears to be little doubt that the wage-formula contract between Gen-eral Motors and the International Union of Electrical Workers (IUE) influenced settlements in the rest of the electrical equipment industry from the beginning.[23] It will be remembered that the GM-UAW-IUE settlement in 1948 called for an immediate 11-cent wage increase. With-in a few months most of the electrical industry settled for an 8-per cent increase that varied from 9 to 15 cents and probably averaged about 11 cents. In 1949 the emphasis was on increased insurance benefits in line with the pattern of that year.

The 1950 bargaining in General Electric and Westinghouse had not been concluded when the Korean action began. In spite of the prece-dent set by the GM-IUE wage-formula contract, neither of the other two major companies adopted this approach. General Electric did adopt a one-year contract with a "one-shot" cost-of-living adjustment review on March 1, 1951. This produced a 9-cent adjustment, which was fol-lowed by Westinghouse. In September 1951 GE gave an additional cost-of-living increase to offset price changes since March and added a 2.5 per cent increase in wages in lieu of an increase based on a rise in pro-ductivity. Westinghouse matched the change. These wage changes re-flect the effect of the GM-IUE formula that was in operation at the time. The Wage Stabilization Board permitted the GM formula to function during the control period. The increases produced by the GM-IUE formula were spread to other companies in the electrical in-dustry on the ground that a "tandem" relationship had existed between company wage changes in the past.[24]

[23] The IUE is the union chartered by the then-CIO after the separation of the United Electrical Workers (UE) from the CIO in 1949. General Motors workers have been represented by the IUE while both unions have substantial representa-tion in General Electric and Westinghouse.

[24] See Arthur M. Ross, "Productivity and Wage Control," *Industrial and Labor Relations Review* (January 1954).

This pattern continued in 1952 as the GM-IUE wage change totaled 8 cents—4 cents each from the escalator adjustment and the annual improvement factor—by June. In September, General Electric and Westinghouse gave increases that averaged an estimated 8.7 cents per hour.

Although wage controls ended in 1953, the tandem relationship continued to influence settlements. The 1953 General Electric settlement was estimated at "over 5 cents" in a year when General Motors gave a 5-cent improvement factor raise. In 1954 the General Electric raise was estimated at "about 5 cents" again. (In both 1953 and 1954 the quarterly price adjustments at General Motors offset one another, so that the 5-cent improvement factor provided the yardstick of comparison.)

It would be an oversimplification to try to explain the General Electric-Westinghouse settlements solely in terms of following a General Motors pattern. General Electric and Westinghouse do the major share of their business in fields in which the GM electrical divisions are noncompetitive. Wage pressures in this case are applied by the union and are reinforced by the existence of active union rivalry. Both the General Motors and the General Electric-Westinghouse settlements were part of national patterns, but the GM contracts dating from 1950 were the independent variable in the situation. General Electric and Westinghouse could be described as "passive followers"[25] of the wage-formula pattern during the period 1948 to 1955; that is, they continued their usual bargaining system, matching the gains already achieved by the GM-IUE group.

As reported earlier, GE and the IUE launched the era of the wage formula in electrical equipment with a five-year contract in August 1955. Westinghouse adopted an essentially similar contract after a lengthy strike. (Beginning in 1955, a pattern of "jockeying" between GE and Westinghouse seems to have increased in importance.)

Like the companies in the steel industry, General Electric views its formula-type contract as an experiment with a different approach to wage determination. The principles of the productivity wage policy are not cited as a rationale for the electrical industry contracts, at least not by the major companies.

The provisions of the wage clauses reflected this lack of concern with the official philosophy. The cost-of-living adjustment was a quarterly

[25] Benson Soffer contributes this phrase and its definition in "On Union Rivalries and the Minimum Differentiation of Wage Patterns," *Review of Economics and Statistics* (February 1959), p. 56.

one, tied to the Consumer Price Index in the familiar fashion. The annual wage increases were set at 3 per cent for 1955, 1956, and 1957, and at approximately 3.5 per cent for 1958 and 1959. According to a General Electric spokesman, a percentage increase of 3 per cent was required in 1955 to produce the same cents-per-hour increase that the 2.5 per cent gave to General Motors' electrical employees. This indicates that the average wage in General Motors' electrical divisions exceeds that of the electrical industry in general. (It does not necessarily mean that General Motors' wages for comparable jobs are higher, but may reflect a different job mix in General Motors compared with the more diversified General Electric and Westinghouse operations.)[26] GE explained the jump in the annual increase to 3.5 per cent in 1958 and 1959 as being based on a belief that the 1958 automobile negotiations would result in an increase in the annual improvement factor. For its part, the union saw the higher rate for the fourth and fifth years of the contract as the inducement necessary to secure a five- rather than a three-year contract.

The IUE believes that increases in productivity justify increases in wages, but it is reluctant to accept the economy-wide rate of increase as the appropriate standard for a wage policy. It believes that the higher rate assumed to be characteristic of its industry would be more appropriate.

For reasons already noted, it is difficult to compare the record of the major companies in the electrical industry while under the formula contracts with their pre-1955 experience. Since the GM-IUE contracts had been essentially the same as the GM-UAW contracts and since the GE and Westinghouse settlements can be related fairly closely to the GM-IUE pattern, some inferences about wage relationships pre- and post-1955 and between autos and electrical equipment can be drawn.

General Electric and Westinghouse have already been described as "passive followers" of the automobile pattern, matching it in size after a time lag. Although the correspondence is not exact, in general, the pre-1955 wage adjustments of the major electrical equipment producers approximated those of autos and GM-IUE in cents-per-hour terms.

[26] Of the seven subgroups making up the electrical machinery industry, companies producing "electrical equipment for vehicles" pay the highest wages, followed by those making electrical generating equipment and electrical appliances. GM's production is concentrated in the first and third of these classifications. See the Monthly Labor Review (November 1960), Table C-1.

Since average wages in the electrical industry are lower than in autos, it appears that, even before the adoption of formula-type contracts, the major electrical machinery producers were probably raising basic wage rates at a somewhat higher annual percentage rate than was the motor vehicle industry.

This judgment can be only tentative since the Bureau of Labor Statistics average hourly earnings series for the electrical industry has actually risen less rapidly than that of the automobile industry. (See Table 2.) Because it is difficult to tell whether the trend in industry-wide earnings is representative of that in individual companies of the electrical industry, the conclusion in the last paragraph is based on a direct comparison of wage settlements when these are available. It is possible, however, because of changes in the composition of employment and because of the system of wage administration used, that earnings in General Electric and Westinghouse rose less rapidly in percentage terms than did base rates.

Because of the passive character of the relationship, the adjustments lagged some months behind the automobile changes and occurred less frequently because of the quarterly price escalator in the latter industry. Even if the net change in wage rates in cents-per-hour were the same, the time lag in adjustment reduced substantially the total cost of the adjustments to the electrical companies.

Repeating the steel companies' practice, GE and Westinghouse built the pre-1955 rate of wage increase into their five-year wage formula contract and even improved on it in the last two years, when the annual increase rose from 3 to 3.5 per cent. They then added the cost-of-living escalator as the price of a long-term contract. Just as in steel, the cost of this arrangement was substantial. In addition, the total wage cost of the 1955 settlements was increased because the quarterly cost-of-living escalator and the scheduled annual increases eliminated some of the time lags that had characterized the earlier system of wage bargaining.

When the five-year contracts ended in the fall of 1960, GE proposed a new contract that abandoned the cost-of-living escalator and called for scheduled wage increases in the future but not at annual intervals. This was an attempt to retain the advantages of long-term contracts without the uncertainty and potential cost of the price escalator. More important, perhaps, was the provision for an eighteen-month period between wage increases—an apparent attempt to break the annual wage increase pattern. The union demanded the retention of the cost-of-living escalator and annual increases but, after a strike against GE, yielded on both issues. In essence, General Electric abandoned the formula approach, offered increases of approximately the same size as formerly but reduced their cost substantially by spacing them at eighteen-month rather than twelve-month intervals during the three-year contract. Westinghouse settled without a strike on terms similar to those described.

Other Industries

A detailed analysis of the experience of the other major industries that have experimented with the formula approach would add little to the above picture. In the typical case the adoption of formulas was a pragmatic, pattern-following decision with little evidence of a basic agreement on a long-term policy.

The long-term contracts in the midwestern trucking agreements negotiated in 1955 and running until 1961 call for semiannual cost-of-living adjustments and annual wage increases of 8 and 7 cents an hour. Annual increases of this magnitude are the same as, or less than, the average increases that were negotiated elsewhere in the years in which these contracts have been in effect. In spite of the additional raises produced by the operation of the cost-of-living escalator, the wage record of the Teamsters union in recent years suggests that in this case the formula may have held wages below what they otherwise might have been.

In 1960 the railroad industry abandoned the experiment with wage formulas that it launched in November 1956. Collective bargaining in this industry is of a highly specialized nature because of the effects of the Railway Labor Act. Contracts usually have not had definite terminal dates, but are reopened on an *ad hoc* basis. Wage bargaining is a long drawn-out process, typically involving the use of a form of voluntary arbitration as the final means of reaching a settlement. Perhaps because of the protracted character of the adjustment process, the unions seem very interested in cost-of-living escalators during periods of rising prices, abandoning them when prices appear to be stabilizing. Both the operating and the nonoperating unions adopted cost-of-living escalators in 1951. The operating unions dropped theirs in 1953, when prices fell, and re-established them as part of the three-year wage-formula settlement in November 1956. The nonoperating unions dropped their cost-of-living escalators in December 1954, to return to them in 1956. The 1956 contracts called for semiannual wage-price adjustments and 7-cent annual increases in three-year contracts. This was a somewhat larger cents-per-hour increase than had characterized past settlements. The wage disputes in 1960 were settled by arbitration or emergency board awards for two-step increases that reduce the rate of wage increase below that produced by the formula contracts.[27] In addition, the cost-of-living escalator was abandoned. The jettisoning of formula-type contracts in this industry may turn out to be relatively permanent since government intervention in their industrial relations disputes has become almost routine for the railroads and their unions since World War II. Given the railroads' present economic circumstances, both sides may feel that the wage-setting procedures of the Railway Labor Act are preferable to contracts scheduling wage increases at specified dates in the future.

In the meatpacking industry, the major companies replaced their 1956 wage-formula agreements with new two-year contracts in 1959. Contracts in this industry have provided for semiannual cost-of-living changes and annual increases in the 7- to 8-cent range. In percentage terms this would be approximately 3 per cent of earnings. Apparently both the union and the companies feel that the wage-formula approach is a satisfactory way of handling the wage issue.

Summary

Viewed in retrospect, the record of the wage-formula system in the major companies indicates that its original innovators and most consistent users have made the system work reasonably well. Most of the imitators have been considerably less successful with this approach.

While individual collective bargaining relationships are subject to a

---

[27] It should be mentioned that, in discussions with the writer, representatives of the industry expressed the belief that the wage formula contracts had not changed the pattern of wage behavior from what they believed would have prevailed in any event. As the text indicates, the writer is dubious of this contention.

multitude of influences, the principal factors responsible for this situation seem to be these:

1. *Timing.* The original 1948 wage-formula contract was introduced early in the postwar period before the idea of yearly increases in wages became widely accepted in collective bargaining. Scheduling increases in real wages several years in advance had an appeal in 1948 that has dimmed as annual raises became commonplace. At least as important was the fact that at the time the GM offer was made, there was no 1948 "going annual increase" pattern that influenced the size of the settlement. In fact, there was an abundance of tough "hold-the-line" talk. In this context the 11-cent immediate increase provided in the contract looked attractive. The relatively low 2-per cent annual improvement factor increase became established as part of the over-all package.

By 1955, when the technique spread outside the UAW sphere of influence, the concession of an annual increase in wages had lost its trading value in bargaining. The companies adopting the system uniformly appear to have extrapolated the wage-increase pattern established in annual bargaining throughout the term of their multi-year contracts. Since the multi-year contract is typically of greater benefit to management, the length of the contract came to be one more bargainable issue for which something must be paid. A cost-of-living escalator, in addition to annual increases equal to, or higher than, those of the immediate past, was the price paid for the multi-year agreement. When prices began their post-1955 rise, continuing through the 1958 recession, disenchantment set in.

2. *Union attitudes.* The United Automobile Workers is one of the more "socially conscious" American unions. The often-expressed philosophy and objectives of the UAW make it more susceptible to the argument that the economy-wide rate of increase in productivity is a proper standard for wage policy. This is not to suggest that Walter Reuther and the Automobile Workers are likely to be carried away by a quixotic devotion to principle that would be uncharacteristic of American labor leaders in general. In an important sense, the union's acceptance of the wage-formula policy represents a well-thought-out long-range strategy. The union is willing to trust to its strength at the periodic renegotiations of the long-term contracts to make additional gains and has done well on balance. Nevertheless, there are few other unions in this country that would or could agree to a contract running for five

years that geared wages to the productivity gains of the community as a whole.

In essence, the experience with the formulas points up a simple lesson. Changes in the externals of the collective bargaining situation are unlikely by themselves to have a major impact on the underlying bargaining relationship. The provisions of the wage-formula contracts reflected the balance of power in bargaining in specific companies and unions. This basic relationship is not permanent and unchanging, and factors such as the form, length, and public rationale of a contract system may be used to introduce change into the situation. This requires that the parties develop their over-all strategy in a coordinated fashion with specific steps toward identified long-range goals, and that they pursue this strategy vigorously and consistently. At least some, if not most, of the companies that experimented with wage formulas did not meet these conditions.

An Evaluation of the Formula Approach

At the conclusion of Chapter 4 it was argued that an assessment of the wage formula in practice should consider two questions: (1) whether perhaps the policy was adopted in areas in which productivity was rising more rapidly than the average while below-average sectors of the economy tended to hammer out their settlements in less visible fashion and (2) whether the performance record of the formulas might not compare favorably with the alternatives that actually were available. This section examines these questions.

Unfortunately, the data needed to answer definitively questions like these are not available. With regard to the first, the only industries involved in the wage-formula pattern for which generally accepted measures of productivity trends are available are basic steel, electrical machinery, and railroads. Tables 3 and 2 show an annual postwar productivity increase of 2.8 per cent for steel and 3.1 for the total private economy when the comparisons are made in terms of output per manhours paid for of all employees. The rate of increase in output per production worker man-hour is substantially higher in steel (3.4 per cent), but presumably the comparable figure for the private economy would also be higher.

Data have recently become available for increases in productivity in the electrical machinery industry.[28] From 1947 to 1958 inclusive, output per production worker man-hour increased at an average annual rate of 4.4 per cent. Output per total worker man-hour increased substantially less, or at about 3.0 per cent per year. Both of these rates, but particularly the former, are higher than the comparable rates for steel. The rate of increase in output per man-hour paid for of all employees in the electrical industry is about equal to the same figure for the private economy.

The BLS publishes output per man-hour of all hourly-basis employees of Class I railroads.[29] Between 1948 and 1958 this series increased at an average annual rate of 4.7 per cent. This rate is substantially higher than that of productivity increases for the economy as a whole for all employees and also substantially higher than increases in output per production worker man-hour in steel.

There are no published data on the rate of increase in productivity in automobiles, meatpacking, and trucking. The average observer would probably assume that the rate of productivity increase in autos exceeded that for the economy in general, and this could very well be true of all three of these industries. This casual assumption could be more easily accepted if it were not that the same belief exists about the steel industry, where it seems to be unjustified.

It seems plausible to hold that the formula system has been concentrated in the more technologically progressive areas of the economy, but the data necessary to prove this hypothesis are not at hand.[30]

Answering the question whether other systems of wage fixing would have yielded results preferable to those produced by wage formulas is

[28] Harold M. Levinson, *Postwar Movement of Prices and Wages in Manufacturing Industries,* Study Paper No. 21, Study of Employment, Growth, and Price Levels, Joint Economic Committee (1960), p. 45.

[29] *Indexes of Output per Man-Hour for Selected Industries, 1919 to 1958* (U. S. Bureau of Labor Statistics, April 1959) (processed).

[30] A rudimentary calculation of trends in output per employee for General Electric can be made from data in the company's annual reports. The percentage increase in sales billed was computed for 1959 relative to 1948, this figure was deflated by the percentage price change for General Electric products, and the result was deflated by the percentage increase in the average number of employees. (The company publishes a product price index.)

For what it is worth, this rough-and-ready calculation produced an annual rate of increase in output per man-hour of all employees of 3.9 per cent per year. Note that the terminal years are slightly different from those used by Levinson.

another impossible task. Since wages generally, including wages under formula-type contracts, increased somewhat more rapidly than the feasible rate during the period under consideration, "preferable" will be interpreted to mean a less rapid rate of wage increase—although many economists might object to this definition.

There are two different contexts in which this question could be analyzed with some hope of reaching tentative conclusions. One approach would be to assess the wage record of the companies and industries with formula contracts both before and after adoption of the system. In the industry sections of this chapter some opinions have already been expressed on this matter. Briefly, it appears that in automobiles since 1948, and possibly midwestern trucking since 1955, the formula approach has produced a rate of increase in earnings no greater than, and possibly even slightly less than, that which would have resulted from annual bargaining. In steel, railroads, and electrical equipment, the wage formula may have increased the rate of change in wages largely because the long-term contracts in steel and electrical equipment eliminated a bargaining session at the bottom of the 1958 recession and because in the railroads the 1956 contracts insulated the unions from the effects of a long-term decline in railroad earnings. In electrical machinery the situation was worsened by a formula-style contract that provided benefits exceeding the pre-escalation pattern. No one can know whether a continuation of annual bargaining would have produced settlements in the years 1955-60 that matched the substantial increases in the Consumer Price Index that occurred, and also provided annual increases roughly equal to, or higher than, the average for the immediately preceding years in the face of the 1958 recession.

The basic issue posed by this approach to assessing the results of wage escalation can be illustrated by an example from the record of the formula contract in steel. During the first year of the 1956 contract, the workers received an initial increase of about 10 cents in 1956 plus a total of 7 cents in cost-of-living adjustments during the next year, or an over-all increase of about 17 cents. During the second year, the total was 18 cents, made up of a 9-cent annual increase in 1957 and another 9 cents from the wage-price escalator during the following year. The record of the third year is confused because 4 cents due from the operation of the escalator from January 1, 1959 to July 1, 1959 was a casualty of the strike over the new contract so that the increase actually realized during 1958-59 was only 10 cents. Would annual bargaining on wages have produced 17- and 18-cent increases in direct wages in 1956 and 1957 or the 14 cents that would have been the cost of the 1958 year had the formula-type contract been renewed without a strike in 1959? The answer can only be an educated guess.

The record of annual bargaining shows that during the Korean inflation, the steel industry gave two 16-cent wage increases in December 1950 and July 1952. The 1953 settlement was 8.5 cents, 1954, 5 cents, and 1955, 15 cents. In this writer's opinion, it is unlikely that annual bargaining during the years 1956-59 would have yielded results equal to those gained under steel's version of the formula in the circumstances of the times.

Another approach to the problem of comparing wage formulas with alternative systems of wage setting is to compare wage behavior in industries or companies using different bargaining methods. This procedure is open to the fundamental objection that attributing all variations in behavior to this cause obviously assigns an exaggerated importance to differences in forms of bargaining. One way of minimizing this objection would be to try to compare industries that are related or are similar to one another in certain wage-influencing characteristics. This has already been done in this chapter where the wage results in the automobile, steel, and electrical equipment industries were reviewed in detail. Other industries that have been used for this purpose in other studies are rubber, farm implements, and aluminum.[31]

Studies of this type usually conclude that related industries have experienced rates of wage increase equal to, or greater than, those found in industries using the formula approach. This is seen in part as the result of a tendency for wage-formula contracts to establish a floor under annual increases during recessions while setting no limits to the increases negotiated in annual bargaining in prosperous periods. On the

---

[31] The most complete study of this type is reported in Benson Soffer, "The Effects of Recent Long-Term Wage Agreements on General Wage Level Movements: 1950-1957," *Quarterly Journal of Economics* (February 1959), pp. 36-60. See also Soffer, "On Union Rivalries and the Minimum Differentiation of Wage Patterns," *Review of Economics and Statistics* (February 1959), pp. 53-61. Soffer concludes that, on balance, the wage formula acted to increase the rate of wage changes in general.

For a similar approach, see J. W. Garbarino, "The Economic Significance of Automatic Wage Adjustments," in Davey *et al.* (eds.), *New Dimensions in Collective Bargaining.*

surface some of these comparisons might be interpreted to indicate that wage formulas have yielded a lower rate of increase, but the argument is that the higher rates in nonescalated industries are themselves a by-product of the operation of the formula contracts where they are in force. Most of the evidence is thus of dubious value in comparative analysis of the two systems of adjustment.

As an alternative approach, the operation of the two systems of adjusting wages as they have operated in successive time periods during which their reciprocal influence might be expected to have been greatest can be examined.

Earlier in this chapter, the opinion was expressed that in the years 1948-50, the GM-UAW contract had little influence on collective bargaining developments. Over this two-year period, the settlements in Ford and Chrysler approximated those in GM but apparently not as a result of the pattern-setting effect of the latter settlements.

Turning to a later period, it is sometimes argued that the experience of the Korean inflationary period from mid-1950 to 1953 was dominated by the automobile wage-formula pattern. In fact, most of the contracts negotiated did not adopt the formula but used a cost-of-living escalator only. The popularity of this device in periods of inflation has often been demonstrated both here and abroad, and the importance of the existence of the GM-UAW example in bringing about its widespread adoption is a debatable point. Pressures to prevent substantial drops in real wages would have been formidable in any event. In addition, the contingent nature of wage increases that depend on prior increases in prices makes the cost-of-living escalator preferable to actual wage adjustments adopted in anticipation of future price increases. (This point is discussed further in Chapter 6.)

A more important influence of the GM-UAW contract on developments during the Korean action was the role that the existence of long-term contracts with annual improvement factors played in pressuring the Wage Stabilization Board to legitimatize increases in other wages. It was argued that private settlements reached prior to the Board's existence should not be voided and that increases that matched productivity gains were not inflationary. The argument that such raises contribute to inflation by raising demand, even if they do not raise costs, was countered by General Motors and the Automobile Workers by the contention that demand pressures should be attacked by tax

policy rather than wage policy. In any event, given the limited character of the mobilization and the economic sophistication of the parties, it can be argued that another set of pressures would have been
operative had the productivity claim not been readily at hand. Other
producer groups were able to protect their position under the wage
and price stabilization program with considerable effectiveness.

The 1954 recession has been widely cited as an example of the floor
effect of the wage formula. At the bottom of the recession, the 5-cent
improvement factor increase in June 1954 apparently strongly influenced that year's wage pattern. The Steelworkers negotiated a 5-cent
agreement with relatively little difficulty in that year in the face of declining consumer prices and low operating rates in the steel industry.
The Bureau of National Affairs reports that the modal settlement in
1954 was in the 4- to 6-cent range for all contracts reported to them.[32]

In evaluating this situation the crucial question is whether the 1954
pattern would have been significantly different in the absence of the
automobile industry's wage-formula contracts. It may be that 1954
would have been the first postwar year in which no increase in wages or
other benefits would have been negotiated. The reader is reminded that
during the 1949 recession annual bargaining produced a pattern of pension and insurance benefits estimated to cost 10 cents an hour. There is
no question but that the exact figure and the exact form of the typical
1954 increase—5 cents in direct wages—was undoubtedly the result of
the pattern set by the formula. It is at least possible, however, that, in
the absence of the formulas, an increase would still have occurred, an
increase that might have been 3 cents or, conceivably, 7 cents.

This evaluation of the formula-in-practice might be summed up in
the following points:

1. There is considerable evidence that the various wage formulas
have tended to produce a rate of increase in total wage costs that has
exceeded the feasible rate of wage increase for the economy as a whole
where they have been in operation.

2. There is some fragmentary indication that wage formulas have
tended to be concentrated in the areas of the economy that are experi-
encing above-average increases in productivity, but the evidence is
speculative and cannot be conclusive.

[32] Bureau of National Affairs, *Collective Bargaining Negotiations and Contracts,*
18:51-89.

3. In some of the industries in which this system of wage setting was adopted it is probable that wages rose no faster than would otherwise have been the case.

4. In other sectors in which the system was used after 1955, it appears that the experiments with wage formulas led to a more rapid rate of wage increase than might otherwise have occurred. Quantitatively, these sectors involve more workers than those referred to in (3). On balance, therefore, the wage formula and its by-product contracts probably raised the rate of wage increase during the years 1955-60, particularly during the 1958 recession.

5. There undoubtedly has been some tendency for wage increases in the sectors using annual scheduled increases to influence wage changes in the other sectors through the floor effect, but this factor has often been exaggerated in importance.

6

Wage Policy in Perspective

IN THE PRECEDING chapters the formula wage policy has been examined from a number of points of view. The objectives which it was designed to achieve, the assumptions on which it is based, the criticisms that have been directed at it, and its operations in practice all have been reviewed. At various stages, judgments as to one aspect or another have been rendered. At this point it is appropriate to attempt to place the policy in perspective and to advance an over-all assessment of its significance.

In making an over-all assessment of the significance of the formula wage policy, it is important to realize that both management and the union are vitally interested in the process by which agreement is reached as well as in the terms of the agreement itself. It can be argued that, as an institution, the union in many instances may be even more interested in the process of agreement than it is in the results of that process. The fact that long-term agreements reduce the degree of participation of the union in the process of agreement is one reason why management has had to pay a "price" for such a contract.

As a technique for the resolution of conflict, collective bargaining is a relationship between organizations, and many aspects of this relationship inevitably become institutionalized as the parties engage in negotiations and other types of organized interaction over the years. The individual company-union or industry-union industrial relations patterns that result from this process differ in many respects. Several analysts of industrial relations have tried to arrange these patterns into classification systems according to their fundamental characteristics. While the characterizations of the various authors differ in terminology, they typically include the equivalent of the four categories of active hostility, competition, containment, and active cooperation.

"Active hostility" refers to a situation in which management is actively resisting the establishment of collective bargaining or attempting aggressively to eliminate it if a foothold has been secured. "Competition" exists when collective bargaining is established throughout most of the company in question, but management has not accepted its permanence and is vigorously but "peacefully" competing with the union for the complete loyalty of the employees in order to demonstrate the superfluity of the union. "Containment" refers to a relationship in which the permanence and importance of collective bargaining is accepted by management, and the company concentrates on limiting the area of concessions and the intensity of conflict. "Cooperation" indicates a policy of active collaboration between union and management on a broad and open-ended set of problems, including some that usually are outside the scope of collective bargaining.

In Chapter 2 the formula wage policy was pictured as a technique for implementing a policy of containment and stabilizing a relationship that was accepted as long-term if not permanent. The goals attributed to the General Motors management were the containment of conflict in terms of frequency and scope, the reduction of the risk of outside intervention in the affairs of the company, and, in general, the stabilizing of all aspects of the collective bargaining relationship, including possibly the identity of the union leadership. These goals were to be attained while keeping the economic costs of the policy within manageable limits. In the case of the United Automobile Workers, the policy guaranteed them two of the three goals of their long-range wage policy. It assured the worker of frequent adjustment of wages to offset price changes and also an annual increase in real wages. It gave the union the opportunity to bargain at periodic intervals for the third goal, a larger share of national or company income.

The major companies adopting the wage-formula pattern in the mid-fifties seem to have had less well articulated policy objectives. In most instances the collective bargaining relationship would also be described as one of containment. Many observers would maintain that one or more of the companies in question may have seen the long-term formula-type contract as part of a policy of competition rather than containment. With its aid, the role of the union as the necessary omnipresent watchdog for the interests of the workers might be minimized. In general, however, the companies seem to have been impressed with the over-all results of the operation of the formula in the automobile industry and simply to have decided to experiment with this approach. As noted in Chapter 5, important changes in the industrial relations environment had occurred since 1948, and the price at which long-term contracts were attainable had gone up compared to that paid for the original one in the automobile industry. If consumer prices had remained stable during the years after 1955, the gains in decreased conflict would probably have been adjudged worth the price paid. As events worked out, the success of the experiment has been seriously questioned.

Not only have the companies directly involved been re-examining the situation, but outside observers have raised questions as to the desirability of the system. In Chapters 3 and 4, the major issues raised by the critics of the formula approach to wage policy have been discussed at considerable length. Although many of the specific points were found to be in need of modification and some were rejected altogether, the final result was a conclusion that a simple wage formula with two variables could not be applied throughout the economy.

There is general agreement that, on an economy-wide basis, the relationship between the rate of increase in real wages and the rate of increase in productivity is a critical one in assessing the performance of an economic system. This relationship need not be one of perfect correspondence in timing and magnitude of change nor need it be one of correspondence between long-term averages. The economy might well survive a systematic divergence in these trends over substantial periods of time and, in fact, may have already done so. Even at the level of generality at which this kind of discussion is carried on—i.e., for the "economy as a whole"—the concepts of "real wages" and "productivity" have been demonstrated to be uncomfortably complex when a rigorous formulation capable of statistical manipulation is made. When the same line of reasoning is carried from the level of aggregative economic analysis to that of a wage policy for a particular company, the problems multiply rapidly.

Many economists would argue that, having pointed out the difficulty of formulating a desirable wage policy at the economy-wide level, the dangers in applying valid general principles to specific cases, and the strong pressures distorting even proper application of valid principles, their professional duty is done. Believing in specialization and the division of labor, they would trespass no further into the field of policy making in industrial relations. It is hardly surprising that economists have seldom gone beyond pointing out the weaknesses of wage formulas as a technique of determing wage adjustments. The wage formula is only one aspect of collective bargaining, a system of wage determination that has proven difficult to integrate into orthodox economic theory and one that serves important noneconomic values and functions. Occasionally arguments against wage formulas will be found on examination to be arguments against setting wages by collective bargaining. Examples are criticisms of the uniformity of adjustments, the special problems posed for marginal firms, and the problems caused by interunion rivalry in wage settlements. These situations exist with or without formulas.

The parties to collective bargaining are not likely to be impressed by counsels to avoid a particular system of wage adjustment unless they know of, or have pointed out to them, alternatives that are superior. This is not to say that critical assessment that does not simultaneously provide superior alternatives is not useful. Those engaged in industrial relations are notoriously pragmatic and are not prone to consider the long-term consequences of their actions. The pressures on them make them particularly likely to imitate established patterns. There should be frequent outside appraisal that tests their policies, not only in the light of their own objectives but of community objectives as well.

The results of the appraisal in this study can be summarized as follows:

1. In the United States the years since World War II have seen collective bargaining evolve from a relatively untried technique for resolving conflict for most of the economy to a well-articulated method of resolving industrial relations issues at the production-worker level.

2. This evolution has included continuing experimentation in the form, the techniques, and the structure of bargaining. Some of the strongest pressures operative during this period have been in the direction of developing stable, long-term contractual relationships, particularly in the strategic power centers of industrial relations. One of the most important examples of experimentation is the formula approach to wage policy, designed to permit negotiation of long-term contracts.

3. The results of the experiment with the formula wage policy and its offshoots suggest that:

a. The policy, considered by itself, is not appropriate as a national wage policy although it has contributed importantly to informal consensus on the general outlines of such a policy.

b. Although it cannot be applied indiscriminately throughout the economy, the system has worked reasonably well under certain circumstances.

c. The effectiveness of the policy must be judged in the light of the probable results of the available alternatives, as well as the objectives of the parties as they themselves see them and the objectives of the community.

4. Collective bargaining relationships are continuing to evolve, and other experiments involving the modification of existing practices and the development of new ones will be attempted.

It would be helpful to review the major alternative policies as to the form and duration of collective bargaining agreements in order to try to identify the circumstances in which specific alternative practices would be appropriate. The following objectives are assumed: (a) a continued reliance on private settlement of industrial relations issues; (b) a continued institutionalization of industrial conflict; (c) a rise in real wages for the economy as a whole at a rate roughly equivalent to the rate of increase in productivity over-all; (d) differential rates of increase among occupational groups, based primarily on labor demand and supply factors, tempered by considerations of social equity for substandard earners; and (e) over-all price stability.

Alternative Collective Bargaining Policies

As to the form and duration of the collective bargaining agreement, there are six principal alternatives.

Contracts of Indefinite Duration

In certain industries in the United States (for example, coal, railroads) collective bargaining contracts without a definite terminal date have been negotiated. The contracts have been reopenable under certain conditions at the option of one or the other party. The impression seems current among students of industrial relations that contracts of this type are more prevalent in certain foreign countries, such as Great Britain, than they are in the United States. A reading of the history of the older American collective bargaining relationships suggests that contracts of indefinite duration may have been more prevalent in the past (for example, the twenties) than they are in contemporary times.[1]

The predominance of contracts with a definite term in American industrial relations at least since the thirties probably stems mainly from a desire on the part of management for stability in union-management relations during a period when a fairly continuous expansion of the area of bargaining has been under way. Management has wanted to avoid the possibility of virtually continuous bargaining as the new function was being integrated into operations. Unions have been willing to accede to periods of consolidation while maintaining an atmosphere of potential improvement through the advance scheduling of renegotiation.

It is entirely possible that contracts of indefinite duration could become more common in the future. As of 1962 there is little evidence that such a development is in the offing for a number of years. The same conclusion seems justified in the case of multi-year contracts without reopenings or some form of automatic wage adjustment machinery. For this reason these alternatives will not be discussed further at this time.

Annual Bargaining

If economists followed the logic of traditional micro-economic theory, they would probably call for short-term contracts with frequent renegotiation to reflect changing economic conditions in individual companies. Many unions probably share this preference, though for different reasons. (But note that unions also may be reluctant to reopen the whole range of nonwage issues annually.) In Chapter 2 the conditions that have caused management to take the lead in pressing for multi-year agreements have been described. In Chapter 5 it was

[1] Of the 287 major collective bargaining agreements on file at the Bureau of Labor Statistics that would be effective on January 1, 1959, only 4 had no fixed term. "Contract Developments Scheduled in 1959," *Monthly Labor Review* (December 1958), p. 1350, Table 1.

pointed out that the overwhelming majority of major agreements in 1958-59 ran for more than one year and that a large number of the employees covered were scheduled to receive wage increases specified in advance.

There are circumstances, however, in which annual bargaining would be desirable, either from the standpoint of the parties concerned or of the economy as a whole. These include situations in which the fundamental balance of bargaining power is in a state of uncertainty or of rapid change. A long-term agreement negotiated when one or the other party holds an overwhelming temporary preponderance of bargaining strength, for one reason or another, is likely to be unsound either in an economic sense or from the point of view of long-run organizational relationships. A long-term contract calling for unusually high wage increases during its lifetime carries the seeds of future economic difficulty and establishes a pattern that is difficult to break without serious repercussions on labor-management or internal union relationships. A long-term contract that reflects unusually depressed conditions in an industry may seem like a short-run gain for management, but may produce a legacy of discontent and mistrust that wipes out these transitory benefits.

Unions typically resist the negotiation of long-term contracts that reflect their low bargaining strength during periods of depression, preferring to sign a short agreement and to live to fight another day. Management has sometimes been less careful in avoiding the negotiation of long-term agreements reflecting prosperity conditions that may be temporary. Examples are not difficult to find and can be discovered among the formula-type agreements discussed earlier. It would be very difficult for a management that has been signing long-term agreements over a period of years to change this pattern and switch to one-year contracts when a renegotiation occurs during a period of high-level boom. Even though a new multi-year contract is negotiated under these conditions, however, the essential element of an annually bargained settlement can be attained if the boom-inspired pressures are expressed in an above-average settlement limited to the first year of the contract with the settlements for future years following the precedents established in the past. In effect, this has been the pattern in the automobile industry. The 1955 boom settlement, for example, held direct wage increases for 1955 and future years fairly well within the limits imposed by the logic of the productivity wage policy and diverted pressures to a substantial fringe package.

Another situation in which annual bargaining may be desirable occurs when an industry may appear to be destined to be a "depressed industry" for the foreseeable future. Under these circumstances, a long-term contract that takes account of the apparent realities of the economic conditions by publicly promulgating a policy of low wage increases or no wage increases for a number of years might be unpalatable to both parties.

Multi-Year Contracts with Annual Wage Reopenings

This type of contract is very similar to annual bargaining except that the range of issues is very much narrowed. The decline in the number of one-year contracts in recent years can be explained largely by the fact that a wide range of nonwage issues, such as seniority systems, have become stabilized and no longer are a source of frequent disagreement.

There is one important point to be made about this type of contract. By narrowing the range of issues that can be introduced into bargaining, the possibility of a work stoppage is reduced. To be effective, a strike or a threat of a strike must command widespread support from the union membership. Particularly when wages are relatively high, a package of demands may need to be assembled to assure support from the various interest groups in the union. A reopening limited in scope makes assembling such a package much more difficult.[2]

It is interesting to speculate on the outcome of the 1959 steel negotiations had they taken place under a reopening agreement limiting them to wages only and had the companies' anti-inflation case not foundered on the working rules issue.

With this sometimes important exception, the multi-year contract with annual wage reopenings is on all fours with annual bargaining, and the comments made there apply here as well.

[2] This point was brought to the attention of the writer by David Lasser of the IUE in discussing the difficulty of mounting a strike threat against GE in 1958, when the contract limited the reopening of that year to employment security issues.

Annual and Multi-Year Contracts with
Cost-of-Living Adjustment Clauses

Under ordinary circumstances, cost-of-living escalators are seldom used in annual bargaining since the price changes that are expected to occur over a one-year period are usually not large enough to warrant much interest in this device. During periods when economic conditions are unsettled and rapid price changes are anticipated (for example, during the Korean emergency), even short-term contracts may provide for wage-price escalators or for frequent reopenings to review the effects of price changes and presumably to adjust wages to take account of them.

The principal reason for discussing this alternative is to point out once more that a formal cost-of-living escalator clause may have positive value under these circumstances as well as in the instances when multi-year contracts with annual wage increases are negotiated. If as a result of the inflationary price anticipations held by the wage negotiators, the wage adjustment includes an offset for expected future increases in prices, the inflationary expectations are made self-realizing. In these circumstances, the contingent nature of the cost-of-living escalator and the fact that its size is directly related to the price changes that do occur may make its use desirable. In its absence, even if the negotiators underestimate the expected increase in prices and build in only a partial offset, the impact of this settlement adds to the immediate inflationary pressure.

Something like this may have occurred during the Korean hostilities, but more important examples are some of the multi-year contracts negotiated in the early years of the "age of escalation," 1956-57. During this period, contracts of three and five years in length with no wage-price escalators, but with annual increases of 5 to 8 per cent of the base year rates, were negotiated, for example, in the construction industry. Increases of this magnitude programmed into the future almost certainly contained an implicit adjustment for expected price increases. Whether the predictions were justified or not, the immediate effect was inflationary and tended to make them self-realizing predictions.

A further advantage of cost-of-living adjustments under these circumstances is that there is a possibility that they may operate at least to a limited extent in a downward as well as an upward direction. In addition, cost-of-living allowances are not usually included in the base rates for incentive purposes. Negotiated wage increases, even when they occur after the fact as a result of a cost-of-living review, are frozen into base rates, are virtually impossible to retrieve in the event of price declines, and often become part of base rates immediately.

The advantages of cost-of-living clauses accrue only when the use of the system is coupled with a basic wage increase that does not include an implicit inflation-offset factor. The addition of a wage-price escalator to a settlement that already creates inflationary pressure produces the built-in inflation situation much commented on in popular discussion and analyzed in Chapter 4.

To round out the discussion, an earlier chapter noted another example of a situation in which a cost-of-living escalator may prove to be helpful. A company in difficult financial straits may be able to negotiate a low- or no-increase wage settlement, or even a wage decrease if the workers are protected against an unexpected decline in real wages by the inclusion of a cost-of-living escalator. This implies that the company does not expect consumer prices to increase substantially and is willing to assume the relatively small risk of a substantial cost-of-living adjustment to achieve an inexpensive basic settlement. In a major crisis, even a small risk may not be acceptable.

In general, it appears that the situations in which the cost-of-living clause has positive value are what might be called "limited emergencies" that fall short of being major crises for a firm or the economy. If a major crisis for the economy is defined as one in which consumer living standards are going to be reduced significantly, then wage-price escalators are likely to be economically undesirable. This is, of course, true as well of all other similar mechanisms designed to protect the real value of various forms of income, and a policy on cost-of-living escalators must be formulated as part of an effective limitation on the operation of all such schemes, or it will be politically unacceptable. Tax policy is the preferred method of distributing a general reduction in living standards.[3] Wage-price escalators are so direct and efficient a

---

[3] As a sidelight, it is interesting to note that the inclusion of certain types of taxes, primarily state and local taxes, in the prices used in calculating the CPI makes the wage-price escalator a device for diluting fiscal policy by influencing the incidence of these taxes. This factor is not of major importance at present, but it has a growing impact and could become important in the future.

technique of protection that some over-all control of their use is likely to be necessary.

Multi-Year Contracts with Scheduled Wage Increases

During the latter half of the decade of the fifties, a substantial growth occurred in the coverage of multi-year contracts that scheduled wage increases to take effect in the future without using cost-of-living escalators. They appear to have come to include about half as many workers as were under formula-type contracts containing both escalators and annual increases.[4]

From the standpoint of the employer, these contracts have some major advantages. They share with formula contracts the benefits of eliminating conflict and strife over the terms of new agreements for long periods of time. If one agrees with Professor Boulding that, "In the study of collective bargaining, sufficient attention has not been given to the fact that bargaining itself is for a great many people a disagreeable, even immoral occupation, and that it is always time consuming . . ." then the prevalence of these two types of contracts can be seen as demonstrating that "bargaining . . . tends to die out in an advanced economy."[5]

Compared with formula-type contracts, agreements limiting themselves to scheduled future increases without escalators have an important advantage in that they make the trend of labor costs predictable for the period of the contract. The achievement of the twin goals of stability of relationships and predictability of costs makes this form of agreement very attractive to employers. In a labor-management relationship that appears to have arrived at a stable balance of bargaining power for the foreseeable future, it is tempting to abandon the "guaranteed annual argument" and adopt a long-term agreement.

Unfortunately for management, the union is less interested in reducing the frequency of wage bargaining in the typical case. Unions are organizations for which bargaining is not a necessary evil, but instead is their principal function, the economic service which they perform for their members. It is the activity by which they demonstrate their

---

[4] *Monthly Labor Review* (December 1960), p. 1257.

[5] Kenneth E. Boulding, *The Organizational Revolution* (Harper, 1953), p. 100.

importance and through which they fulfill their role in society. The effect of this is to convert long-term contracts that reduce the opportunities for bargaining into concessions that must in turn be bargained away from the union. The longer the term of a contract, the greater the risk that developments in the industry or in the economy or the gains won by other unions will make what originally seemed a satisfactory settlement appear to have been a serious tactical error. As a result, a long-term contract must usually be purchased at a price.

There is another reason why a premium must usually be paid for a multi-year contract of this type. Such an agreement is in effect a contract for the future delivery of hours of labor services at a fixed price. Because the "spot" price of the labor at the time of delivery is often expected to reflect any changes in consumer prices that may occur before that time, someone must bear the risk of possible price fluctuations. Since in the memory of the great majority of the present generation of workers these changes have been in an upward direction, a collective bargaining contract without a wage-price escalator appears to shift the burden of uncertainty about future consumer prices to the workers and to the union as their bargaining representative. Under present circumstances, a premium must be paid to induce them to assume this risk, the size of the premium reflecting the price expectations of the parties.

In this type of contract, the price usually takes one of two forms. It may be paid as a larger gain in the first year of the contract, as either a larger wage increase or a new fringe benefit. Multi-year contracts often specify a higher initial wage increase than is scheduled for future years, and the difference can be regarded as the cost of the long-term contract. Alternatively, each of the settlements during the lifetime of the contract may be higher than the typical settlement in the years immediately preceding the signing of the long-term agreement.

In analyzing this version of the long-term contract, it will be helpful to start by assuming that expectations of consumer price changes are neutral in that they do not materially affect the decisions of the parties.

This pattern of bargaining has proven attractive to industries characterized by strong, stable unionism and a strong preference for predictability of labor costs. Perhaps the outstanding example is the construction industry. In construction, collective bargaining relationships in the organized areas are of long standing, and contractual provisions have been codified over many years. Demand for the product is inelastic, wages have a record of substantial, steady rise regardless of the form of bargaining, and much of the work is performed under a system of contract bidding and takes months or years to complete. Under these circumstances, long-term contracts with periodic wage increases appear as a relatively painless method of handling a potential problem area.

Of course, the public has no objection to stability, predictability, or industrial peace unless it is purchased at the cost of inflationary wage settlements. It may appear at first glance that the typical contract of this kind does call for inflationary rates of wage increase. The picture is complicated by the fact that in some instances they have merely formalized rates of increase not very different from what might have been expected to result from annual bargaining. Management in these cases is "cooperating with the inevitable," and the outside observer who asks them to bargain annually and try to reduce this rate is in the position of saying, "Let's you and him fight."

To an individual company or to a group of companies the added cost of a somewhat higher rate of wage increase may be less than the losses resulting from one or more strikes. The social cost of industrial strife may be low or negligible to the community as a whole but quite high to individual companies. Contrariwise, the social cost of industrial peace purchased at a price may be relatively high while the private cost to an individual company may be low. "Tight money" represents an attempt to increase the private cost of inflationary wage settlements, but this remedy is a blunt weapon that may have its own social costs in terms of reduced employment and production.

A further complication in evaluating individual contracts of this type is that there is no unambiguous standard to which the negotiated rate of wage increase can be compared to establish its inflationary character. Once again, it should be remembered that, unless all wages are to change proportionately, some should go up at a rate greater than the "feasible" rate or the rate that is noninflationary for the economy as a whole.[6] Here labor supply and demand factors can help in judging a particular settlement, but it should be recognized that this is not a simple solution.

[6] For a discussion of the feasible rate of wage increase, see Chapter 3.

In general, the feasible rate of wage increase for the economy as a whole should be the basic standard, and the burden of justifying above-average increases should be on the company and union involved. In the present institutional context, however, it is not surprising that some employers succumb to the temptation to choose the relatively easy way out.

When the assumption that price expectations are neutral in their effects on the size of the settlements called for in this type of contract is relaxed, the situation becomes more serious. The point has been made repeatedly that, if consumer prices are expected to rise during the term of the agreement and a safety factor is added to the scheduled increases as an offset, the result is certainly undesirable from the point of view of the economy. If such a practice is at all widespread, the social cost may exceed the apparent private cost to at least some of the individual bargaining units. If the negotiators underestimate the rate of price increase or do not fully compensate for it for some other reason, a long-term contract with annual wage increases may appear to be a bargain for the company. The effect of all such contracts considered separately or as a group, however, is immediately inflationary.

From the standpoint of individual companies, their two major alternatives when prices are expected to rise are (1) to turn to annual bargaining or periodic wage reviews with their potential disrupting effects and unpredictable costs or (2) to add a cost-of-living adjustment clause to the contract. The latter choice also makes future labor costs unpredictable. Under these circumstances, many companies choose to gamble on outguessing the trend in prices in establishing their future increases, arguing that the impact on prices of their settlement alone will be negligible.

From the point of view of the economy as a whole, the following conclusions seem to be indicated on the basis of this discussion:

1. Long-term contracts with scheduled wage increases should be avoided if the increases include an offset for anticipated price changes.

2. When price expectations are neutral, such contracts may be workable:

    a. when they can be negotiated while keeping the long-run rate of wage increase over successive contracts no higher than the feasible rate, or

    b. when, if wages rise faster than the feasible rate, the rate of increase in productivity for all employees is greater than the rate of wage increase so that some price reduction is at least possible, or

c. when, if wages rise faster than the feasible rate, the rate of increase in wages is required to meet a bona fide shortage of labor for the occupations involved.

If price changes occur that have not been anticipated, the appropriate policy for dealing with this situation cannot be stipulated without considering the reasons for the price increase, the impact on living standards in the economy, the economic position of the companies involved, the level of wages in the bargaining units, and other factors.

Multi-Year Contracts with Wage Formulas

The last type of collective bargaining contract to be discussed is the most complex—those contracts combining wage-price adjustments with annual increases that are the principal focus of this study. Compared with the simpler multi-year agreements with only scheduled wage increase, these contracts have permitted companies to secure long-term agreements but without predictable labor costs. In the language of the previous section, they are contracts for the future delivery of labor services at a fixed *real* wage rate but at a *money* wage rate that varies with changes in consumer prices. In essence, the risk of future price increases is borne by the company rather than the worker. The long-term feature of the contract is purchased at a price that is not only unknown in advance, but that is also beyond the control of the individual company.

As noted in Chapter 2, General Motors, the leading exponent of this approach to collective bargaining, justifies the assumption of this risk by arguing that the future price of labor services will be adjusted to take account of upward changes in consumer prices in any event. If this argument is accepted, the cost to the company is measured not by the size of the cost-of-living adjustment but by the addition to the wage bill over the years that results from reducing any time lag that might otherwise have occurred. If multi-year contracts with scheduled increases, but no wage-price link, include premiums either to secure union agreement to a long-term contract or to offset anticipated price changes, it is entirely possible that their total wage cost could exceed the total wage cost of a formula-style contract even during periods of price inflation.

Of course, if inflation does not occur, the formula contract is the cheaper.

The kind of calculation that is required to approximate the total cost of a wage-formula contract is illustrated in Chapter 5, where the wage cost of the 1948-50 GM-UAW contract was estimated to have been roughly equal to the cost of the Ford and Chrysler contracts. In another study the writer developed data that can be used to estimate the total direct wage costs of GM's settlements compared with U. S. Steel's from 1948 to 1956. In this case GM's total costs appear to have been below U. S. Steel's by an average of about 0.6 of a cent for each hour worked, or, very roughly, about $100 per full-time employee equivalent for the eight years.[7] (Once again, the reader is reminded that this differential need not be due in any way to the differences in the type of bargaining that prevailed in these two companies.)

The following points sum up the comparison between multi-year contracts with and without cost-of-living escalators. (Where appropriate, the statements assume the comparison of two situations in which the balance of bargaining power, however this might be measured, is the same.)

1. The inclusion of cost-of-living escalators does not, by itself, start a price inflation. They do contribute a secondary inflationary pressure:

a. if the annual increases in the formula contracts are of a size sufficient to trigger a rise in consumer prices, or

b. if inflation results from the operation of any one of the other numerous possible causes, including wage increases negotiated in other sectors of the economy.

2. If no price inflation occurs, wage-formula contracts are cheaper than a nonescalated, multi-year contract if the nonescalated agreement's future increases include any premium to induce the union to sign or to compensate for expected price increases.

3. If no price inflation occurs and no premiums are paid to secure agreement to the nonescalated contract, the total costs of the two contracts will be unaffected by the difference in the form of the contract.

[7] See J. W. Garbarino, "The Economic Significance of Automatic Wage Adjustments," in Harold Davey et al. (eds.), New Dimensions in Collective Bargaining (Harper, 1959), pp. 164-67. The $100 figure results from multiplying 0.6 cents by 40 hours per week, 13 weeks per quarter, and 32 quarters. No allowance is made for the added costs of U.S. Steel's incentive system.

4. If price inflation occurs, the total cost of the wage-formula contracts compared to nonescalated contracts depends on the size of the premium (if any) paid to secure the nonescalated contract and the time pattern of the increases generated by the cost-of-living escalator.

5. If price inflation occurs and no premium is paid to secure a nonescalated contract, the latter contract is the cheaper unless the union is able in subsequent contracts to more than make up the reduction in real wage increase that resulted from the price inflation.

This catalog makes it clear that the crucial questions in comparing these two types of contracts are first, the terms on which nonescalated long-term contracts are available and second, the validity of the assumption that unions can effectively make up inflation-induced losses in real wages and also make new gains in real wages through periodic bargaining without the aid of formal cost-of-living escalator clauses. Although, as President Charles E. Wilson of General Motors pointed out, over the long run money wages in general have increased enough to offset price increases and also to raise real wages, there is no assurance that they will in the future, and, more important, there are certain time periods and certain sectors of the economy in which they have not done so in the past.

This is an appropriate point at which to consider the major modification of the formula approach exemplified by the 1960 steel contract. The contract contained a cost-of-living escalator, but it was limited in the upward direction to an increase of 3 cents or about 1.5 points of the Consumer Price Index per year. (This ignores complications introduced by the insurance cost offset.) This set a maximum to the risk of future price increases that was assumed by the companies and shifted to the workers the burden of any further increase that might occur. By past standards this was a narrow range of variation. The general principle of limited liability embodied in this approach has much to be said for it. It can be argued that an individual company should not expose itself to the risk of price increases that might be considered "unusual" or "abnormal" in extent. A rate of price increase above a certain level might well be regarded as a symptom of serious economic difficulty and be considered an occasion for a re-evaluation of wage policy. It should be recognized, however, that this reduces the attraction of a long-term contract to the union, and this may result in a compensating benefit being added elsewhere. In the case of the steel contract the industry chose to expend bargaining strength to win the limited escalator rather than some other concession.

It has also been suggested that the Consumer Price Index adjustments might be scheduled to occur no oftener than at six-month intervals and that the size of the CPI change needed to set off a wage change might be larger. On this latter point, the reader is reminded that if the unit of wage change is to be 1 cent, the change in the CPI required to trigger a change in wages will grow progressively smaller. This results from the fact that, if money wages are to rise faster than prices in order to raise real wages, the value of the price index/money wage ratio that determines the size of the adjustment factor (see Chapter 2) will shrink. In addition, if prices increase secularly, the effect of periodically shifting the price index to later base periods also reduces the size of the adjustment factor. (By 1960 these two trends had reduced the size of the change in the CPI equivalent to a 1-cent change in wages from 1.14 to 0.5 in the GM-UAW contract.)

Both of the proposed changes would reduce the sensitivity of wages to price changes and would probably be desirable on balance. Again, it should be recognized that these changes will appear as losses to the workers if price increases are expected in the future.

Compared with wage-formula contracts, the multi-year contract with wage reopenings, the other major practical alternative, provides neither freedom from the threat of a work stoppage nor predictability of labor costs. Its chief virtue is potential flexibility in adjusting to changing economic conditions and to the changing fortunes of individual companies. This could be an important advantage from the standpoint of both the community and the companies involved. This flexibility, however, is limited substantially by the strength of pressures toward pattern-following in various sectors of the economy. One segment of the public typically exaggerates the freedom of action available to individual bargaining units while another segment typically exaggerates the rigidity of pattern-following, but there is no question that commitments to a particular series of wage increases for up to five years into the future mean an important loss of potential freedom of choice. The widespread adoption of multi-year contracts with one form or another of scheduled future wage increases after 1953, suggests that many companies believed the gains from stability would exceed any benefits they could realistically expect to reap from the potential flexibility of annual reopenings. The 1962 steel agreement will be an interesting experiment in this area.

Summary

This discussion of the principal characteristics of the major alternative forms of collective bargaining contracts indicates that the choice among them should be related to the objective facts of a given collective bargaining situation, to expectations about general economic conditions, particularly trends in consumer prices, to expectations as to the behavior of prices and productivity in a particular company compared to the economy as a whole, and to expectations about the trend of wages in a particular company under the alternative types of contracts.

Annual contracts are appropriate when the collective bargaining relationship is unstable, the long-term balance of power is uncertain, or an economic crisis for the economy or the particular company exists or is highly probable.

Multi-year contracts with wage-reopenings are appropriate under the same circumstances. They have tended to replace one-year contracts as nonwage elements of the bargaining relationship have become stabilized. On economic grounds alone and from the standpoint of the community, this type of bargaining is preferable to the other possibilities in most instances because of the potential flexibility it provides. Current wage settlements can reflect the current economic environment, not the expectations held at the time a contract was negotiated years in the past.

Multi-year contracts with scheduled wage increases provide a company with both stability in relationships and predictability in costs. These benefits may, in the absence of an economic crisis, offset the private costs in loss of flexibility and possible premium settlements. They are most likely to appear when companies face strong, stable unions and are convinced that periodic increases are inevitable anyway. Problems arise when the scheduled increases exceed productivity increases or anticipate price increases.

Multi-year contracts with both scheduled wage increases and cost-of-living adjustments provide a company with stability at the cost of the risk of consumer price increases. As an offset, the company may be able to negotiate a somewhat smaller annual increase than would be possible without the protection provided by the escalator.

Employers who place a high value on stability and order in industrial relations, who are optimistic about the future level of business activity and their own company's prospects, and who are pessimistic about the possibility of avoiding substantial, regular increases in wages in any event, are likely to be strongly attracted to one or the other type of long-term contract with automatic wage adjustments.

Wage Policy and the Future

As of early 1962, it is tempting to minimize the importance of wage formulas as a technique of wage-setting throughout most of the economy during the next several years. The railroad and the electrical industries have abandoned the practice, and the steel industry has negotiated an emasculated version of the formula. Continuance of the system in a major area of the economy was assured when the automobile industry renegotiated its contracts in 1961.

Considering the burden of the criticisms that have been levied at the system both as a general policy and in some of the specific cases discussed in Chapter 5, the reduction of the area of application of wage formulas might be hailed as a positive gain. In the short run this may be a valid assessment of the situation, but in the long run it might well be a mistake to minimize the direct and indirect influence of the formula approach to wage policy or its importance for the future of wage determination. This statement is based on the belief that the alternative to this system, at least in the major power centers of collective bargaining, is not likely to be annual wage negotiations but multiyear contracts with scheduled wage increases.

Considered as a social process, collective bargaining is often seen as a long-run conflict relationship in which the parties evolve orderly and systematic solutions to a wide variety of issues as a result of continued personal and institutional interaction.[8] Viewing the institution of

[8] Robert Dubin, *Working Union-Management Relations* (Prentice-Hall, 1958), pp. 240-49.

collective bargaining in this way, it seems unrealistic to assume that one major area of dispute—wages—will continue to be handled indefinitely on the basis of annual tests of pure bargaining power. It would seem more realistic to assume that there will be an institutionalization of conflict over wages rather than to adopt the somewhat romantic assumption that repeated *ad hoc* bargaining can occur without the development of standards by which analytical processes can be applied to the resolution of this type of dispute as they have been applied to others.

Obvious candidates for such standards are changes in living costs, changes in productivity, comparable wages, the economic condition of the firm, and labor supply and demand factors. This is not to suggest that devices such as the GM wage formula will be elaborated by adding more terms to the formula to take account of the effects of other criteria. The wage formula approach or its equivalent is more likely to survive in areas of the economy in which productivity change is satisfactory and firms are prosperous and confident of the future. Labor supply factors can be taken into consideration through special increases to specific occupational groups in addition to the formula gains, as has been done for skilled workers in certain of the automobile contracts.

The criteria of wage determination used in the wage formula and those noted earlier have been used for many years in wage negotiation. Their use is completely compatible with annual bargaining, where the arguments they represent have long been employed with considerable imagination and with a studied lack of consistency in the interests of expediency. They will of course continue to be used under these circumstances and in this fashion. The argument here is that, for reasons stressed in Chapter 2, certain major company and industry negotiations are subject to tremendous pressures to minimize the occasions of full-scale collective bargaining. The principal means presently at hand to accomplish this is the multi-year contract which, for the foreseeable future, requires the inclusion of some form of "automatic" wage adjustment machinery. The effort to develop such machinery leads toward the systematic application of the wage criteria in customary use, e.g., as in the GM wage formula.

In the years immediately ahead, the multi-year contract with periodic wage increases but without automatic living cost adjustments, will probably grow in popularity relative to the combination of these two evidenced in the current wage formulas. Particularly if wage formula contracts remain prominently on display, as in the automobile industry, the settlements in the other multi-year contracts will certainly be influenced by the same criteria.

In fact, the most important effect of the GM-UAW experiment with the wage formula has been to give the "productivity wage policy" something approaching the status of a rudimentary national wage policy. The main features of the formula or productivity wage policy are a belief that the gains in living standards made possible by increasing productivity should be distributed by raising money wages and that these gains should be scheduled automatically so as to offset changes in prices and provide regular increases based on projected increases in productivity. Probably no other single factor has been so influential in making an annual money wage increase virtually ubiquitous for the organized worker in the United States as the 1948 GM wage formula agreement and its successors. There also are few other single factors more responsible for the intense interest in relatively minute variations of the Consumer Price Index and the conversion of such changes into issues in wage setting.

For reasons discussed at various points in this study, most economists probably regard the widespread acceptance of the doctrine of the annual wage increase as an article of faith in the American workers' creed as undesirable on balance. On the credit side of the ledger of the formula version of wage policy, there should be entered the less widespread but latent notion that productivity increases not only *permit* real wage increases but that they *limit* the size of these increases for the economy as a whole (neglecting certain international trade considerations). As the concepts involved are refined and sharpened, the net effect of the wage policy may well be beneficial if it focuses attention on the need to reconcile wage increases above the economy-wide average with the productivity mystique. This would be particularly important should the U. S. experience a period during which the rate of increase in living standards characteristic of the past were to decrease. The debate stirred by the experiments with the wage formula can be used to improve the possibilities of social control of industrial relations through the pressure of an informed public opinion. It is fashionable for the experts to dismiss the effects of exhortation and public persuasion on the realities of collective bargaining situations. It is hard to believe, however, that the negotiators for the Steelworkers' union would not testify to the strength of the impact of the barrage of public pronouncements on the potential inflationary effects of wage settlements from various public figures in the spring and early summer of 1959. It is also hard to believe that the Kennedy Administration's policy of trying to hold the price line has been as innocuous as many observers appear to believe. If direct control of wages and prices is to be avoided and if the application of indirect methods of control by monetary stringency is to be limited by considerations of economic performance, then any addition to the arsenal of social control mechanisms is welcome.

The 1962 *Annual Report of the Council of Economic Advisers* includes a discussion of "guideposts for noninflationary wage and price behavior" (pages 185-90), which is noteworthy as an attempt to go beyond the usual call for relating wage changes to productivity changes in a generalized way. The problem of implementing this prescription is recognized, and some "modifications" of the general guides are proposed in order to establish differential patterns of wage changes in specific labor-management negotiations. In general, the Council stresses factors considered in Chapter 4 of this study. The Council's remarks are implicitly couched in terms of real wage changes, and no consideration is given to the mechanics of taking account of general price movements should they occur. This statement is a step in the direction of prescriptive wage policy as distinct from efforts to evaluate the inflationary impact of wage behavior after the fact. The passage from a review of results to the statement of normative principles in advance of wage settlements seems to be inevitable.

During the 1960's it may well be that the concern with the possibility of wage inflation may shift from the highly visible negotiations in industries such as steel and automobiles to the much larger number of relatively "invisible" settlements in smaller manufacturing and particularly in nonmanufacturing industries. Protected from the glare of the spotlights focused on "administered-price" industries, protected from the rigors of competition outside limited regional product markets, protected from national publicity through the mass media by the geographical limits to any individual settlement, protected from analysis by the lack of easily available data, negotiations in these sectors are conducted quietly in an atmosphere of "mature" collective bargaining. The back pages of almost any metropolitan newspaper report a constant series of settlements by construction workers, teamsters, retail clerks, restaurant workers, machinists, warehousemen, operating engineers, etc., many of which produce wage gains of impressive proportions. The cumulative effect of hundreds of these settlements could well be of major importance for price behavior. If the publicity for the principles of the productivity wage policy results in its application in these areas, the effects could be salutary. Surely a discussion of wages, prices, profits, and productivity in, say, the construction or the trucking industry would be of more value than a repeat of past discussions that will almost certainly feature future negotiations in steel or autos.

Leaving the actual and potential influence of the general principles of the productivity wage policy to return to an assessment of the experience with specific wage-formula contracts, it should be stressed that the difficulty with some of the attempts to use this approach has been a failure to achieve the necessary pre-conditions for its success. The decision to try a formula approach does not change the basic balance of bargaining power. The parameters built into the wage-formula contracts, including the original GM-UAW contracts, are not only the result of the appeal of the logic of the system; they also reflect the bargaining position of the parties. When the bargaining situation is such that above-average, possibly inflationary, wage increases would have resulted from other types of contractual arrangements, the adoption of a formula approach to wage getting will not change the result substantially. Over the long run, in the general case, the concepts of the wage policy on which the wage formula is based may operate to influence the results of collective bargaining settlements. In any specific negotiation, the introduction of these ideas is unlikely to have much impact except as they exploit a general climate favorable to their acceptance. This general climate may require long preparation and careful manipulation to create. Where the balance of bargaining power permits the negotiation of wage formula contracts with a rate of real wage increase roughly in line with the feasible rate or where a divergence from this rate coincides with above-average rates of productivity increase or true shortages of labor, these contracts are likely to be workable from the standpoint of both the community and the company involved.

As the decade of the 1960's began, the 1955-56 converts to the formula approach to wage bargaining were slipping off the band wagon. Once again the automobile industry-UAW groups make up the principal bloc of adherents to the system.

The companies abandoning the practice, often in the face of considerable union opposition, seem to be trying to achieve the following objectives:

1. *Elimination of the escalator clause.* The unpredictable character of the cost associated with the use of the escalator has already been noted. A more subtle factor may also be at work in that some of the companies trying to drop the clause have been accepting the costs of "hard" bargaining to reduce the level of scheduled increases being negotiated. The escalator represents a potential cost "leakage" that may negate the gains won in head-to-head bargaining.

2. *Reduction in the size of the scheduled wage increases.* Earlier much of the dissatisfaction of the late-comers to the formula system was ascribed to the practice of giving larger annual increases than the logic of the formula called for or than the automobile group was conceding. Currently the steel industry, for example, appears to be trying hard to reduce the magnitude of these increases.

3. *Elimination of the concept of the annual wage increase.* The most ambitious goal seems to be the attempt to space increases at intervals longer than the calendar year. General Electric made a breakthrough on this front in 1960. The strategy seems to be to offer a substantial immediate increase with another substantial increase scheduled in advance, but more than one year into the future. The union must then make a strike issue not of the size of the immediate increase, not of the size of the future increase, but of the *timing* of the future increase. In some circumstances this can be a sophisticated and successful strategy from the company point of view, despite the cost of exposure to the rigors of annual wage bargaining.

The renegotiation of the automobile-UAW contracts in 1961 does not, of course, imply a permanent commitment to the formula system. The history of this relationship does suggest, however, that it would take a major shift in the balance of bargaining power that was expected to continue over a substantial period to bring about the abandonment of the wage formula. As long as the range of feasible alternatives does not change materially, the formula is likely to survive. The profit-sharing settlement involving American Motors in 1961 represents an attempt to relate the company's wage liability to its economic performance. This may turn out to have some long-term significance but as a complement to rather than as a substitute for the formula increases.

The Steelworkers contract, negotiated in April 1962, took the form of a multi-year agreement with a wage reopening at the end of the first year. This arrangement may represent the beginning of a new phase of collective bargaining relationships. In an earlier section, it was suggested that annual bargaining or its near equivalent, the multi-year contract with annual wage reopenings, can be expected to be favored when ". . . the fundamental balance of bargaining power is in a state of uncertainty or of rapid change. . . ."[9] The cost of the steel industry's long-term contracts with automatic wage adjustments, including the 1960 version, has probably been higher than the industry believes is tolerable over the long run. Long-term contracts with automatic wage adjustments project the bargaining balance of power existing at the time of negotiation into the future. At a period when one or the other party to the conflict believes the momentary balance of power to be unstable, strategy may call for a holding action with a renewal of the duel at a relatively early date. In the steel situation, the parties have chosen to accept the risks of restaging the industry's collective bargaining spectacular with its star-studded supporting cast in 1963.

Whether Republican or Democratic, the national administration's stake in the consequences of wage bargaining suggests continued concern with the criteria used in wage determination. In a real sense, the administration in power has been trying for several years to convert public opinion into an effective force operating on major collective bargaining settlements. The increase in the official or semi-official interest in the appropriateness of particular settlements, as expressed in *ex-post* investigation or discussion, is likely to lead to more explicit formulation of such criteria for *ex-ante* application. A short step in this direction has been taken in the 1962 *Annual Report of the Council of Economic Advisers*, with its "guideposts" for wage and price behavior.

All this suggests that the question of the proper wage policy for the American industrial relations system will be a subject of growing importance.

[9] See page 118. For an elaboration of this approach, see Joseph W. Garbarino, "Bargaining Strategy and the Form of Contracts," *Industrial Relations* (February 1962), pp. 73-88.

Index

Index

Index

141